The Great Eastern Mussel Cookbook

The Great Eastern Mussel Cookbook

Cindy McIntyre & Terence Callery

Good Cooking
Terry

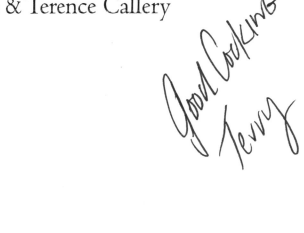

Paul S. Eriksson
Publisher
Forest Dale, Vermont

This book is dedicated to the memory of Mel Pell,
who for a decade tirelessly introduced mussels to
the American public. As Great Eastern's corporate chef
and cooking demonstrator, Mel used humor, enthusiasm,
and intelligence to convert tens of thousands
of consumers into mussel fans.

Photographs by Cindy McIntyre except for the following: P. 6—Phyllis Graber Jensen; P. 27—Scott Wellsandt, *Seafood Leader Magazine*; P. 28, John Sylvester; P. 32 and 38, Great Eastern Mussel Farms.

Illustrations by Jerri Finch except for the following: P. 18, courtesy of GEM; and P. 35, Melani Darrell.

Library of Congress Cataloging-in-Publication Data

McIntyre, Cindy
    The great eastern mussel cookbook / Cindy McIntyre and
Terence Callery.
        p.   cm.
    Includes index.
    ISBN 0-8397-2392-X (paper)
    1. Cookery (Mussels) 2. Mussels. 3. Cookery, International.
I. Callery, Terence. II. Title.
TX754.M98M35   1995
641.6'94—dc20   95-14770
                                CIP

CONTENTS

∞

NUTRITIONAL INFORMATION

MUSSELS ARE VERSATILE for use in menu planning. They make a nice presentation in their shells and add depth to a meal if served whole or chopped. When planning a meal with an emphasis on nutrition, mussels can offer balance, based on their nutritional value.

The Center for Science in the Public Interest has told the country that fish and seafood dishes offer the lowest level of fat and cholesterol of any ethnic meal. According to the Food and Drug Administration's criteria, mussels are an extra-lean meat.

Some definitions:

• **Extra-lean**—contains 5 grams (g) of fat, less than 2 grams of saturated fat, and less than 95 milligrams (mg) of cholesterol per 100 gram (3½ ounce) portion of food.

• **Low-sodium**—main dish products have 140 mg or less sodium per 3½ ounces or 100 g. of food. (Salt is 40 percent sodium and 60 percent chloride.)

• **Low-fat**—main dish products have 3 g. or less total fat per 3½ ounces or 100 g. of food and not more than 30 percent calories from fat.

One pound of mussels, in the shell, yields three and one-half ounces of raw mussel meat or 100 grams. Comparing the nutritional information of 3½ ounces of mussels with the information generally found on food labels for a 2000* calorie diet, we

	3½ ounces (100 g.) mussels (uncooked, raw)	2000 calorie diet (per day)	% Daily Value
Calories	95	2000	4.8
Total fat	2.1 g.	less than 65 g.	3.2
Saturated fat	.5 g.	less than 20 g.	2.5
Cholesterol	55 mg.	less than 300 mg	18
Carbohydrate	2.5 g.	300 g.	1.1
Sodium	284 mg.	less than 2400 mg.	12
Protein	14 g	50 g.	28

viii ᔆ *The Great Eastern Mussel Cookbook*

get the Percentage of Daily Value.

By looking at the percent calculations, one can create a balanced diet with mussels combined with a variety of other foods. At the end of a day, you can add up the percents for the same nutrient, to see how close you come to 100%, thereby meeting the nutritional needs for consuming 2,000* calories per day.

We have rated all the recipes in our book that qualify for "extra-lean", "low-sodium", or "low-fat" status. The criteria for these ratings are figured for 100 gram or 3½ ounce servings. Please note that many of our serving sizes are in excess of 100 grams, so that a recipe may be rated as low sodium, low-fat, or extra-lean and contain more than the allowed amounts due to the larger portion sizes.

— Patricia Hart

Wine with Mussels and Other Seafood

ᔆ

STILL BELIEVE that you can only drink white wine with seafood? Think again. Reds can also work. In fact, all of the old rules about matching the color of wine with food can be thrown out the window. The variety of the grape and how the wine is made (its style) are more important considerations than mere color. A red such as Pinot Noir can be soft, delicate and very subtle. Sauvignon Blanc (a white varietal) can be made in a style that is powerful, heavy and herbaceous and can completely overpower

a delicate fish dish. The key, then, to matching wines with food is to understand a little more about the flavors of wine. Here are a few guidelines that we use in deciding what wine to serve:

• *With briny, salty dishes, serve wines that are off-dry, low in alcohol and without tannins.* If you haven't read much about wine I should stop here for a brief explanation of the terms "off-dry" and "tannins." Off-dry means that the wine has a little bit of residual sugar left in it. If it were completely dry, all of the sugar in the fruit would have been converted to alcohol. Typically off-dry wines are lower in alcohol (10-11 percent by volume) compared to dry wines which can run 12-13 percent. Varietals that fit in the off-dry category are Riesling, Gewurztraminer, Chenin Blanc, and White Zinfandel.

Tannins are those flavors which cause the mouth and tongue to pucker a bit—like when you drink tea which has been brewed too strongly. Tannins occur predominantly in young red wines. A bit of tannin can add interest to wine and food—but too much can be a real turnoff. If you think about adding salt to an already "puckering" tongue you no doubt get the idea that this would not be a very good match. Salty foods, then, are softened by off-dry wines. A completely dry, tannic or oaky wine such as a typical California Chardonnay or Cabernet creates too much of a contrast in the mouth and sets up a battle of flavors in which neither side wins. Mussels by their nature have a salty edge and, in the absence of any other sauce or flavoring, I'd serve a good, chilled Riesling or Gewurztraminer.

• *With high acid dishes, serve a high acid wine.* Exam-

---

* 2000 calories has been selected as a reference amount by the FDA for labeling purposes because it approximates the maintenance calorie requirements targeted for weight reduction.

ples here would be a seviche in which a lot of fresh lemon or lime juice is used to "cook" the fish or a mussel salad with a fresh lemon viniagrette. A young Sauvignon Blanc with good matching acidity and crispness would work well here. Off-dry wines would taste too sweet and strange with such acidic dishes.

• *With rich-tasting dishes, serve a rich white wine or lighter red wine.* A dish of grilled salmon with an herb-butter sauce or mussels in a creamy ginger butter sauce goes wonderfully with a rich, oaky, "fat" California Chardonnay. The safest approach in any food and wine pairing is to put together flavors which complement each other as in these matches. Occasionally, however, contrasting flavors can also work and my preference would be to serve the salmon, for example, with a Pinot Noir, a varietal red usually made with delicacy and not overloaded with tannins. The little bit of tannin helps cut through the fattiness of the fish and sauce.

• *Serve smoked fishes with off-dry, lower alcohol wines.* As with salt (and often smoked fishes are cured with salt,) a Gewurztraminer, Riesling, Chenin Blanc or well-made White Zinfandel softens and rounds the smoke flavors. Crisp, acidic wines seem to clash. For this reason we don't serve sparkling wine or champagne with smoked salmon or mussels, even though this is often touted as a classic combination.

• *Serve deep-fried foods with very crisp, high acid, dry white wines or (surprise!) a good California sparkling wine.* Assuming that the deep frying is done well, i.e. not leaden and oily, the crisp wine seems to enhance the burst of flavor one experiences with good deep-fried food. Seafood can be great with a clean, non-oaked California Chardonnay or French Chablis. If you're

feeling festive, my favorite would be to go with a sparkler. A rich, oaky Chardonnay, most red wines or wines with sweetness just don't work.

• *Serve spicy foods with low-alcohol, off-dry or low-tannin, fruity red wines.* Another surprise—wines can work with your favorite Thai or Latin flavored fish dishes. Be sure they're low-alcohol (higher alcohol tends to accentuate heat) and fresh and fruity. A bit of residual sugar seems to calm the heat and refresh the palate. For whites, try a California Gewurztraminer or Riesling. On the red side, young California Gamay or French Nouveau Beaujolais can work really well here (again helping to debunk the white wine with fish rule!)

• *Don't worry too much about serving the same wine you use in cooking a dish.* Another of the old rules says that you should be sure to serve the same wine with a dish if you've used it in the preparation of that dish. Wine is only one component in a dish, and when it's cooked it both loses its alcohol and marries with the other flavors in the dish—changing it dramatically. Look at the overall flavors in the dish to decide what wine to serve.

Too often we can get intimidated by wine. Part of this is due to the tremendous number of choices that exist, and part of it is due to the tendency to make wine too "precious." Wine is one of the oldest and most basic foods. It is meant to be enjoyed in context with food. Don't be intimidated. Hopefully the guidelines above will encourage you to try and decide what you like. In the final analysis, that's what is important. Drink what you like. It's part of the joy of cooking and eating.

— John Ash

Captain Hubba Bradford and son Adam on the F/V St. George with a full hold of seed mussels

CHAPTER ONE

Mussel Harvesting on the Coast of Maine

HUBBA BRADFORD leans against the desk of the wheelhouse on the *F/V St. George*, animatedly relating sea tales while guiding the fishing boat through lobster buoys in Moosabec Reach off Jonesport, Maine. Cold rain falls, and fog is gathering, and he's got 50,000 pounds of mussels to scrape off the ocean's bottom before he can call it a day.

"There's not a fisheries I haven't done," he says, keeping his keen eye on the drag net full of mussels as it empties into the hold. "I've even gone looking for wrecks." He found one, too. The *Central America* went down off Cape Hatteras in the hurricane of 1902 with a cargo of gold from California mines. Though his crew was unable to salvage the booty, New York financiers later resurrected the treasure from its watery grave.

Hired by Great Eastern five years ago to captain its mussel dragger, the 49-year-old fisherman is quintessential Maine: rugged, rowdy, raucous. Though museling isn't exactly adventure on the high seas, Hubba—or F. Brent Bradford, as he is known in official circles—still keeps things interesting. There's the six-inch thick winter ice to bust over the mussel beds, for instance. And the inevitable groundings and impromptu camping trips on the beach from dragging in shallow water. Not to mention the epithets hurled his way from lobstermen whose traps are accidentally cut, or the golf balls thrown at the *St. George* by another musselman who didn't like the competition.

But Hubba, a former lobsterman and ground fisherman himself, tries to keep a low profile. A Falmouth (southern Maine) native, he's the newcomer in Downeast (northern Maine) territory, where folk are slow to warm up to strangers but extra generous when they do. He's working wild beds with his son Adam, 22, dragging up seed mussels for replanting on a nearby Great Eastern lease site. A lobster boat

Aerial photograph of the F/V St. George *breaking February ice to reach shallow water mussel beds.*

zooms past, its riding sail flapping like a race horse's mane.

"Take a picture," he says. "Boy, I love to see somethin' like that." To him, it is poetry of man, machine and the sea.

Fishing's been in Hubba's blood since his mother bought him his first skiff and lobster traps at age six. One of his fondest memories is a photo of him at age 12 in a Tarzan bathing suit, his mother holding on tight as he bent over hauling a trap. As a kid he tried to get hired onto fishing boats, but nobody would take him. In his heyday, Hubba owned a fleet of three fishing boats, all named after his wife Mary Ann, but when the groundfisheries collapsed in the mid-80s, he sold out.

Hubba sends the mesh drag net 40 feet to the bottom of the overcrowded beds in the Reach, hauling up inch-long mollusks that will be re-harvested 18 months later and two inches longer. Having grown out with less competition for food, these cultivated mussels will have tender meats superior to that of their strictly wild cousins, with fewer pearls and almost no barnacles.

After the drag net empties the mussels into the vessel's hold, Adam guides it back into the water, then begins picking out bycatch. Starfish, sea urchins, an occasional bottom fish, and sea cucumbers are tossed back into the sea. He destroys the hated green crabs, which are mussel predators.

Fog, another hazard of fisheries, is growing thicker, nearly obscuring the bridge to Beals Island. The boat drags up and down the channel, filling the hold. The deck gets muddier and slicker. Adam hoses it off and continues picking out bycatch, rain oozing down the neck of his oilskin. By early afternoon, the last drag "chockablock full" is emptied onto the hold's mountain of glossy black baby mussels. "They're some tough," Hubba says, watching Adam scurry over the mollusks, tossing out starfish. "Man, they take some abuse."

The rain comes down heavier. Hubba squats and squints through the speckled windshield to locate buoys and channel markers as the boat steams an hour north to a nearby island. Six blue buoys marked "Sea Farm" define the 30-acre lease site,

Adam Bradford brings up drag net full of seed mussels

where the Sci-tex readout shows the ocean bottom to be only six feet below—three feet lower than the boat's keel. Designed for waters like these, the *St. George* is the only vessel of its kind in North America, patterned after Dutch draggers.

Adam steers and Hubba works the levers, scooping mussels from the hold into the spreader, funneling them onto a whirling disk that flings them into the water. Checking the map to pick up where they left off the day before, the men criss-cross the lease site, broadcasting seed onto a muddy bottom that has proven viable for cultivation.

When the month-long seeding operation is finished, more than one and a quarter million pounds of wild mussels will reside in new waters. Great Eastern's leaseholds have increased in recent years, and depending on the quality of wild beds, between 10 and 50 percent of the company's catch is cultivated.

"The future of musseling lies in farms," says Hubba, who fears mussels may go the way of other Atlantic fisheries depleted by overfishing and environmental changes.

> "Indeed I am in love with you
> Out all night in the foggy dew,
> Indeed I am in love with you
> Mussels in the corner."
> Traditional song from
> Newfoundland
> "Mussels in the Corner"
>
> ∞

Too, the future of fishing has never been more precarious. "For 25 years it's been nip and tuck," he says of his career. "I didn't see the kids growing up. Because of that, I didn't want them to follow in my footsteps." But the sea got into Adam's blood, and his 18-year-old brother Andrew is studying at the Maine Maritime Academy. "This is the most time I've ever spent with Adam," says Hubba, watching his son clean the deck.

He shifts the levers, squints through the gathering fog, and turns the *St. George* around for home.

Chris Hinck inspects packing room

CHAPTER TWO

MAINE AQUACULTURE:
Planting Seed for Tomorrow's Ocean Harvest

"Mussels are the perfect health food: high in protein and vital minerals such as calcium and iron, low in calories and fat. When it comes to omega-3, the miracle fatty acid found in fish, mussels have more of it than any other shellfish."

— *Seafood Leader*
Sept/Oct 1993

IT WAS DESPISED AND SCORNED, good only for fish bait or fertilizer, if it was good for anything at all. On Cape Cod, a bounty was once paid to have it hauled off the clamming beds. But now it is gold—buried treasure on the muddy bottom of the sea. "It" is the edible blue mussel, *Mytilus edulis*, and its several cousins. This lowly, ubiquitous bivalve has been the Rodney Dangerfield of shellfish, getting "no respect" until recent years, when North Americans began to discover its exquisite taste and low price.

This treasure had long been prized by Europeans and Asians, who have been cultivating mussels for generations. In some areas of France and Belgium, more mussels are eaten per capita than *all* seafoods eaten by Americans. The prized mussel is grown on bamboo poles in Thailand, on thick oak "bouchot" poles in France, from ropes dangling from rafts in Spain, on long-lines in Sweden, and on the ocean bottom in the Netherlands.

It wasn't until the mid-1970s that anyone in America thought mussels worthy enough to cultivate. Now, more than 15 million pounds (shell weight) are farmed by scores of aquaculturists in North America, ranging from California and Puget Sound to Maine and Prince Edward Island, Canada. Hundreds of millions more pounds occur in wild ocean beds, on rocky shores, on pilings, and on the bottoms of boats.

> Mussel culture on hanging ropes began in Spain in 1901 at Tarragona on the Mediterranean coast.
>
> ∞

Why this intensive effort to cultivate what is so abundant in the wild? Exquisite taste, consistency, and quality are the reasons. Mussels are naturally gregarious. And sedentary. They spend their adult lives anchored to their chosen home, eating whatever plankton and detritus happens to float by. There is, however, only so much food to go around, and competition for it keeps most wild mussels—which tend to live in crowded neighborhoods—growing sloooowly.

In addition, those growing in intertidal zones (areas exposed at low tide) are not feeding at all for a good part of each day. Meats may be small and muddy-tasting. Many folk who have eaten wild mussels know that grit, sand and pearls are often unwelcome accompaniments to an otherwise good meal.

Cultivation simply enhances the natural growing conditions of wild mussels, allowing them to be thinned or to be seeded at densities that allow less competition. The result is a faster-growing, thinner-shelled critter with few pearls and sweet, tender meats. Those grown on ropes don't accumulate grit that plagues bottom-dwelling brethren. And cultivated mussels scooped from the ocean floor are placed in purging tanks where they rid themselves of grit and unneeded byssus threads (beards) before they are sold. In short, cultivation takes a good thing and makes it better.

Prior to the first attempts at cultivation, the total U.S. wild harvest reached one million pounds in 1969, mostly from the New England states and New York, and the quality of mussels in the marketplace was poor and inconsistent.

During the U.S. meat boycott in 1973, the Maine Department of Marine Resources in conjunction with the University of New Hampshire and Sea Grant tried to sell the public on this under-utilized resource. A quarter million servings were given out in

Edward Myers, "Grandfather of Maine Mussel Aquaculture"

restaurants, supermarkets, and at special events in New England. Maine's production increased 150 percent, but remained only an "incidental" fishery.

In the United States, mussels were first farmed in the cold, clean waters of Maine in 1973 by Edward Myers, a Princeton graduate who recognized the commercial potential of this "poor man's seafood." His 5-acre Abandoned Farm on the Damariscotta River was partially funded through the Sea Grant Program of the National Oceanic and Atmospheric Administration, which provided money for research related to experimental culture of mussels. The program spurred research and business opportunity on both coasts. Myers's farm grew to nearly 20 acres.

Until Myers turned over the operations to a neighboring aquaculturist in 1993, he was still using the rope-culture method he devised 20 years earlier, keeping production to that of a small cottage industry. Myers is the quintessential Maine "character." His office was in a converted chicken coop; he used a 1924 Maytag washer to declump the mussels; and he dispensed philosophy and wit freely. His rafts, initially made from power poles, were upgraded to old tires filled with chemically inert urethane foam, and are now wooden poles floated by plastic barrels that once contained Coke syrup. Each pole supports 14 ropes, each of which produces about 120 pounds of mussels. At their location seven miles upstream on the Damariscotta River, the waters have a salinity content that equals the inshore waters in the Gulf of Maine.

Myers—like any inventor/entrepreneur—made his share of goofs. At one point, after prodigious kelp settled on the ropes, he was advised to go into the seaweed business instead.

Endicott "Chip" Davison, owner Great Eastern Mussel Farms

In 1977, Yale graduate Endicott "Chip" Davison left the New York District Attorney's office and came to Maine looking for adventure and a higher quality of life. In search of a worthwhile project to sink his teeth into and to help him scratch out a living, he eventually found himself under the employment of Edward Myers. In a 12-hour meeting, Myers explained to Davison the possibilities of starting up a new industry. It wasn't until the last ten minutes of that meeting that Myers cooked up a batch of freshly harvested mussels steamed in their own juices. One taste and Davison was convinced of the great potential of the mussel business.

Over the next several months, Myers and Davison

wrote a business plan to grow mussels commercially in Maine. During this time only small East Coast ethnic communities were eating mussels. A French restaurant, for instance, would put out a call to a seafood wholesaler, who'd call Boston, who'd call a lobster dealer, who'd send someone out to fish a bed of wild mussels. That was the extent of the industry.

After working for a year with Myers at Abandoned Farms, selling to a small clientele of restaurants that wanted Myers's hand-picked mollusks, Davison elected to go out on his own. With a new partner, Frank Simon, he formed his own company—Great Eastern Mussel Farms. They duplicated the rope-culture technique learned from Myers. Mussels were picked at their lease site on the Sheepscot River in Edgecomb, purged off the dock in lobster crates, cleaned and boxed in Simon's basement, then hauled in the back of their pickup to their buyers. They worked long hours for little pay, and market resistance was high.

In the beginning, GEM had two main problems to solve. One was to develop a cheaper technique for growing mussels in Maine. Another was to identify a market willing to pay for the higher costs of a farmed mussel. With this in mind, Davison and Simon drew up a business plan to develop growing techniques and then went up and down the coast of Maine in search of superior quality mussels, for which they paid higher prices to fishermen. These

> "When thou forgivest, the man who has pierced thy heart stands to thee in the relation of the sea-worm, that perforates the shell of the mussel, which, straightaway closes the wound with a pearl."
>
> Jean Paul Richter
>
> ∞

mussels were then cleaned up and made "pot ready" for the market. Then the partners flew around the country trying to peddle them.

"Boston wholesalers would say, 'What are these things? Get them out of my office,'" relates Davison, who was not yet 30 when he began Great Eastern. Needless to say, at that time there was no market in Boston for high-quality mussels. Starting in San Francisco, they eventually bypassed the wholesalers and went directly to restaurants, which liked what they saw. After awhile, restaurant demand was high enough that wholesalers began to take another look.

"Mussels leaving Maine at that time were big, old, ugly wild mussels with pearls, small meats, and barnacles," says Davison." But we knew the day we put our mussels in people's mouths that it would be a good business."

By 1979, there were six mussel farms in the United States, all using rope culture. Four were in Maine, one in Rhode Island, and one in Washington state. The combined harvest was under 30,000 pounds.

In 1980, after traveling throughout Europe investigating the "latest" mussel farming techniques, Davison and Simon decided to try the Dutch bottom-culture method. If this method succeeded in Maine, costs would be dramatically lower than in the rope-culture method. After two years of working with Stonington, Maine fishermen Jack Hamblen and Bob Burgess, the partners found the Dutch method to be successful, producing the same high-quality mussels at much lower costs. Great Eastern then abandoned rope-culture altogether.

In 1982 GEM outgrew its original plant in Edgecomb, Maine and moved to its present location on Long Cove in St. George, near Tenants Harbor. In 1986 the *F/V St. George*, a 65-foot dragger/seeder was built. Designed after Dutch seeding/harvesting vessels, it is still the only vessel of its kind in North America. Four years later Frank Simon left GEM to form another business, although he is still active as an owner and a member of the board of directors. Davison remains as corporation president.

Currently Great Eastern has approximately 100 acres of active mussel farms. GEM leases are located in unpolluted areas northeast of the Kennebec River. This area rarely sees the red tide scourge that occurs for an average of two months every summer in more southerly waters.

The company also fishes "farmed-quality" wild beds that meet its high standards. "The vast majority of mussel beds are unmarketable," says biologist Carter Newell, GEM quality

Carter Newell, Biologist

control and farm manager. Pollution, barnacles, and pearls make them unusable; rocky habitats render them commercially unreachable, and proximity to prime lobstering areas makes some beds unfishable. Additionally, because of state funding cutbacks, some wild beds can be closed as a precaution due to lack of water sampling. Sea farms, says Newell, eliminate these barriers.

Each spring the mussels along the coast of Maine spawn. In some places there is so much seed that a drinking glass could be dipped in the ocean and there would be microscopic seed in every scoop. By July 4th, the seed "sets"— or settles on boat hulls, lobster traps, rocks, and on the ocean bottom. The following April, GEM locates these subtidal ocean beds and then spends the summer transplanting the seed to its aquaculture leaseholds.

After 18-24 months on the farm, the seed grows to a market size of 2¼ to 3 inches in length—ready for harvest. Wild mussels may take 7 to 8 years to reach that size. These fast-growing mussels are then dragged with a metal-meshed net and given an initial washing over the farm area, where mud and any smaller mus-

A SINGLE FEMALE MUSSEL may produce between 8 and 40 million eggs a year.

∞

On the picking belt, a crew removes everything that's not mussel—whelks, periwinkles, broken shells, and rocks.

spected for breakage, the mussels are boxed and shipped via distributors to restaurants and supermarkets throughout North America. Samples of each lot are tested for shelf life, and retained for 2 weeks in the unlikely event of consumer problems. Computer records are kept to track meat yields and other quality control information by lot number. Information is tracked on a database to determine which sites have the best quality mussels. "The meat yield is significantly higher on farms than on wild sites, if seeding densities are managed properly," says biologist Newell.

The maximum aquaculture lease site allowed by the state to a single entity is 150 acres. Applications for lease sites are scrutinized in a public hearing to determine that the site is not a critical habitat for endangered species such as bald eagles, terns, or marine mammals, or is critical to some stage in the life cycle of other species (e.g. lobster shedder holes.) The state wants to be sure the new lease

sels return to the bed. The boat harvests only as much product as the sales force in Tenants Harbor projects it will sell in the next few days. This is in direct contrast to other fisheries which catch as much as they can of wild stocks to sell at fluctuating market prices based on supply and demand.

When mussels arrive at the processing plant, they are placed in 20,000-gallon rewatering tanks for 24 hours to purge out any sand or grit. After being retested in the plant's lab, graded for size and in-

doesn't displace an existing fishery or interfere with navigation. Sometimes objections are based on aesthetics; as the working waterfront becomes gentrified by folk who have often made their livings out-of-state, this becomes an issue more and more.

Although only the leaseholder can use the area for aquaculture, activities such as recreational boating and fishing are allowed. Unlike salmon pens and rafts for rope-cultivated mussels, the only visible indication of a bottom mussel lease are several sea-farm buoys that mark the site boundaries. No chemicals, antibiotics or artificial foods are ever introduced into the mussel lease areas in Maine.

Sustainability of the resource has been an issue since the late '70s. Consultants and scientists even then feared overfishing. "In 1978 I thought we'd run out of mussels in two years," reflects Davison. "The market grew at a horrific pace."

Today, mussels are marvelously abundant, but *quality* beds are getting harder to find, and "ugly" gritty wild mussels are no longer acceptable by the consumer. This trend supports a bright future for

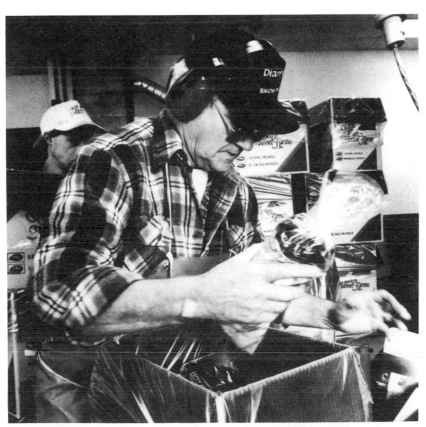

The bags are placed in waxed and lined boxes, ice is put on top, and the boxes are sent to the cooler—a huge refrigerated room that keeps them at the proper temperature until the trucks arrive.

aquaculture. With farmed product comes a consistent high quality product.

Studies show that dragging the sea bottom is environmentally benign in mussel beds. In the wild, over 90 percent of the population in the beds is mussels. Most non-target bycatch is returned to the sea. The animals and plants that live where mussels do are adapted to similar disturbances of tide and storms, and recolonize quickly. In addition, during harvest many small mussels fall through the slats in the rotating mussel washer, effectively reseeding the original bed at a lesser (more desirable) density. These wild beds are then accessible upon maturity to any mussel dragger, not just a particular harvester.

In the first year, GEM halted fishing during the spring and early summer season when mussels were spawning. But the company, anxious to retain markets, began "fishing around the spawn," locating beds that had not yet spawned, and waiting until later in the season to fish the others. Better handling techniques at the plant also decreased the chance that harvested mussels would spawn in the purge tanks, and also increased shelf life. Now GEM harvests and sells year-round.

GEM has come a long way from that 10x20-foot uninsulated pine building on the banks of the Sheepscot River. Production has

Mussels are placed in 20,000-gallon rewatering tanks to purge themselves of sand and grit. The amount of time mussels purge in these tanks depends on the season and water temperature. Because metabolism speeds up in warmer water, their purge times are as little as 12 hours in summer. In winter, they are purged longer, and their shelf life can be as much as 14 days.

grown to over six million pounds, making the company the largest harvester in North America, and the only one engaged in bottom culture. Although GEM harvests both wild and farmed mussels, recently GEM has stepped up its farming effort, dropping three million pounds of seed onto its aquaculture leases in 1994. To ensure top quality distribution, GEM delivers product throughout the Northeast through its own fleet of refrigerated trucks.

The vagaries of nature and the market still create problems for mussel growers. Eiders feast on cultivated beds as readily as they do on rope cultures. These large sea ducks, which were once hunted nearly to extinction, can travel in rafts of 1,000 to 2,000 birds, sometimes wiping out an entire planting of seed. "We lose ten percent of our production to eiders," says biologist Newell. He tries to work *with* nature, rather than against it by selecting seed that is above the size most vulnerable to predators and planting it in an environment that discourages them.

Weather can also wreak havoc, as it did in 1992 when a strong northeaster churned up the sea bottom for over a week on Nantucket Shoals and Monomoy Shoals in Massachusetts and Rhode Island. Mussel beds that were the backbone of the Rhode Island industry were buried under several feet of sand. That fishery now relies on beds that are sometimes infested with pea crabs, tiny crustaceans that live inside the mussel's shell and steal its food. It goes without saying that pea crabs, while entirely edible, are a startling addition to a steaming pot of mussels.

A SEA DUCK can eat five pounds of small mussels a day, swallowing them whole and grinding the shells in their gizzards. A flock of 1,000 to 2,000 eiders can remove over 50,000 pounds of young mollusks a week from a sea farm, and they'll dive as deep as sixty feet to get them in the wild.

Cultivation requires a strategy of science and intuition, uneasy bedfellows. Fishermen have mined the sea for generations without statistics, pronouncements or predictions of meddling academics who have never mended a net or braved a northeaster in a bucking dragger. But Newell has taken laboratory results and applied them in the field, learning from failures and duplicating successes. To explain his work, Newell hauls out reams of research papers: charts on growth rates and water temperature and filtration efficiency and plankton concentrations and so on. "We've broken new ground in researching the ecology of shallow water in Maine," he says. What he has learned on behalf of a commercial enterprise has also benefited science. Much of his pioneering work for Great Eastern has been published in academic papers, and has allowed GEM to develop new techniques and equipment for better efficiency and meat yield.

The biologist works with colleagues all over the world to study mussel cultivation and to swap information. By obtaining grants, he has been able to study mussels feeding on the ocean bottom using a video camera, develop a more efficient boat washer, locate patterns of food availability using aerial and satellite photographs, study the relationship of eelgrass to mussel larvae, and generally figure what makes a mussel happy.

> WHILE MORE than two-thirds of the world's surface is ocean, 99 percent of the world's inhabitable space (in terms of cubic area) is in the sea.
>
> ❧

One study he collaborated on with researchers from the Woods Hole Oceanographic Institution in Massachusetts found that the natural clumping of mussels creates turbulence as water flows over them. These eddies bring plankton down from the top layers of water and increase the mussels' food supply. A lone mussel could not produce this effect, but working together creates a synergy that benefits the colony. For GEM's purposes, Newell discovered that mussels grow better in smaller clumps, because larger patches create a "shadow effect" that deprives those downstream of food.

Then there are those who just go fishing. In

GEM uses three of its own trucks going to Boston, New York, and Montreal

1988-89 a huge bed of wild mussels was found on Nantucket Shoals. "They were dirt cheap, not purged, and had a different taste," says Davison. "They weren't as sweet as the Maine mussel." But these lesser quality bulk mussels found a market, to the detriment of producers selling on a quality reputation. However, Great Eastern had been branding its name on an innovative two-pound retail bag, which featured quality assurances, holes for air and drainage, and recipes on the back. The concept was so successful that other companies copied the bag idea.

Wild mussels, which make up a significant percentage of GEM's harvest, must meet strict standards. Many a fisherman's catch has been placed back in the ocean due to poor quality. This sets Great Eastern apart from many independent wild harvesters who re-fit a lobster boat and mine any bed regardless of quality. Those mussels may be washed off and placed in onion bags for market. Unfortunately, these gritty, poor-quality shellfish can perpetuate the trashy image that plagues mussels. Great Eastern's reputation and success were built upon selectivity, and the fan mail received each week proves again and again that mussels—when handled properly—are a gem of a food.

Mussels are low in calories, fat and cholesterol while high in protein and heart-healthy omega-3 fatty acids. They can be substituted for clams in nearly any recipe, and with skyrocketing prices of clams, mussels have been an attractive alternative. At the Rockland, Maine Lobster Festival in August 1994, 2500 pounds of mussels replaced the traditional steamer clams in the shore dinner. Clam prices were upwards of $120 a bushel, compared to culti-

vated mussels at $30. The decision to replace the venerable clam was influenced not only by price, but by availability. Festival organizers couldn't find the quantities of clams they needed at any price. So they bought mussels.

As the world's population increases, aquaculture will play an increasingly important role in supplying seafood. Mussel aquaculture is particularly productive, yielding between 8,000 and 300,000 pounds of meats per acre. GEM's yield on farmed sites is about 15,000 pounds per acre. Even the richest grass-

Great Eastern's efforts to educate both the seafood buyer and the consumer about mussels have introduced these shellfish to markets that have never tried mussels before.

lands in the United States can produce only about 150 to 200 pounds of beef per acre. Being low on the food chain, mussels expend less energy converting themselves into food than do cattle or predatory fish such as tuna or haddock.

According to the U.S. Department of Agriculture, since 1983 total aquaculture production of all U.S. fisheries rose steadily from 300 million pounds to 700 million pounds. Aquaculture produced more than 17 percent of the world's entire fish supply in 1991. Nearly a quarter of that was shellfish. As world fishery resources become depleted, aquaculture is playing an ever-more important role in assuring the availability of seafood to the consumer.

In the early '70s, the Maine mussel industry made a negligible contribution to the state's economy. Today it provides more than $8 million in income to about 600 Maine residents; this includes the spin-off effects of companies that provide supplies and services to the industry, as well as wages and other income spent within the community.

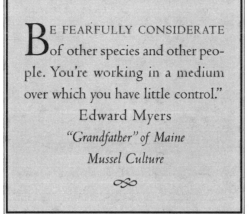

B E FEARFULLY CONSIDERATE of other species and other people. You're working in a medium over which you have little control."
Edward Myers
*"Grandfather" of Maine
Mussel Culture*

∞

In his 1995 inaugural address, Maine's Independent Governor Angus King said, "We must become farmers of the sea, for we have at our edge a field as vast and as fertile as the Great Plains of the Middle West. An aquaculture industry comparable to Norway's would employ 9,000 and help to feed the world."

However you look at it, aquaculture is changing the face of world food production. Great Eastern is on the leading edge of farming this new frontier, turning "trash" into "treasure." Not bad for a once-despised mollusk, is it?

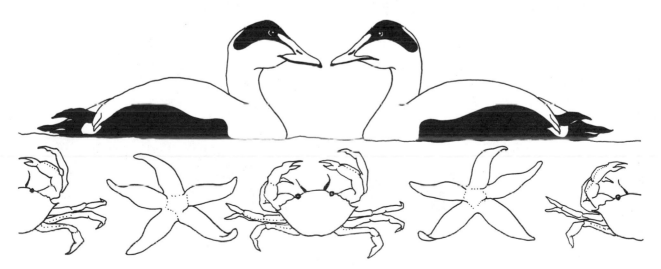

Eider ducks, green crabs and starfish are the main predators of the mussel.

CHAPTER THREE

EVERYTHING YOU WANTED TO KNOW ABOUT MUSSELS

(and Some Things You Didn't)

"Hail, happy shell! from heart-ache ever free!"

S O DID 18TH CENTURY POET George Farewell rhapsodize about the mussel, "this less than reptile" feasting on Neptune's bounty unhindered by human angst. Today's scientists, however, take a less anthropomorphic view, though one no less awed by the mussel's complexity. If it weren't for human interest in eating them, we would still be in the dark ages of musseldom. Instead, there are entire books and reams of scientific papers devoted to edible mussels, and marine biologists can indeed wax rhapsodic when they describe mussel metamorphosis and settlement as it relates to phytoplankton blooms and eelgrass meadows.

In the process of trying to make the mussel useful to humankind, science uncovers some interesting things, things that make you wonder if maybe, just maybe, there isn't some sort of intelligence between those glossy black shells. Under that nerdish molluscan exterior is a highly interesting little critter. Take the beard, for instance. This scour pad-like substance, called the byssus (BISS-us), has gotten the scientific community to spend wads of money trying to figure out how it works. More specifically, scientists want to know how the glue that attaches the byssus to solid objects functions underwater. Surgeons would like to use such a glue in dental and eye surgery, and to reattach fine nerves; the U.S. Navy wants to use it to repair ships without the expense of drydocking them. A repeating string of amino acids has been found to be the key, and companies are now trying to manufacture the glue commercially.

In attaching the byssus, which is its set of anchor lines, the mussel does a tricky little thing with its foot. It creates a plunger-like suction that vacuums the water away from the spot where it wants to place the byssus strand, then it deposits a dab of "pre-adhesive" which cures into a fine thread within minutes. By slightly varying the composition of the pre-adhesive, the threads closest to the shell have extra elasticity to absorb shock. The strands are then coated with a protein varnish. Takes some smarts to figure that all out.

Then there's the foot, from whence the byssus comes. Contrary to popular opinion, mussels *can* skip town on foot. If their neighborhood goes downhill due to changing water quality, they can release their byssus threads and crawl away. However, a mussel striking out alone is asking for trouble. Starfish and green crabs lurk in the shadows, waiting to pick them off. Generally, it is only the young and restless that take a hike; established families aren't too enthused about starting over.

The mantle is the "envelope" that wraps the fleshy part of the mussel. It is responsible for secreting the shell (and annoying pearls), detecting changes in light and motion, storing excess nutrients, and producing the gametes at spawning time. The oils in a lady mussel's eggs turn the mantle orange, and the mantle of the gents is a creamy white.

> THE BYSSUS material produced by mussels is so tough that Greek fishermen would knit fishing gloves from it. The gloves were so durable that they were passed down from father to son.
>
> ∞

Interior anatomy of a mussel. The genus name Mytilus *comes from the Greek "mitilos" for "sea mussel."*

The dark sac in the mussel is the "tummy" or digestive gland—an indicator of the rich phytoplankton (single-celled algae) they have imbibed. Occasionally, during a bloom of *Mesodinium rubrum*, which turns the water red (but is not a poisonous "red tide"), the mussel meats are a reddish color and may have a slight peppery flavor. Indeed, it is known that mussels will have different flavors depending on where they are growing, because of the various types of phytoplankton found in the local waters.

Mussels can exercise some selectivity when it comes to filtering the water for food. Generally, bacteria and organisms smaller than three microns (a micron is $\frac{1}{1000}$ millimeter) are too small to be retained, and particles larger than 200 microns won't pass through the filter. Twenty micron plankton are just right, but if their concentrations are excessive, they could hinder the mussel's ability to process them. A 2½-inch mussel generally filters about 15 gallons of water a day, and in some places where suspended cultivation is being done, one can notice a remarkable clarity in the water immediately downstream from the feeding mussels.

In mussel society, it is polite to eat with mouths open. Rows of cilia on the gills coax the seston, or particulate matter, toward the labial palps and mouth, where the good stuff gets invited in, and the rejected material is pushed out. Some cilia pump the water through the gills, other cilia are the quality control agents, and some transfer the goodies towards the mouth. Enroute, the particles are given a final inspection at the labial palps where an arrangement of ciliated grooves and ridges guide the material either to the mouth, or to the hinterland. Excess feed is passed out of the exhalant siphon as "pseudofeces," and these nutrients produced by mussel waste provide a feedback loop to sustain plankton concentrations.

Inside the digestive system, food is directed and redirected, some of it for further processing. Generally, mussels growing in the front rows of the colony—those that face the current—grow the fastest, and bottom cultivators take this into account when planting seed on a lease site.

It might surprise you to know that mussels have little hearts that pump clear blood, and they have a kidney, a stomach, and a mouth, but like the scarecrow, they haven't got a brain. Makes you wonder how they do all the amazing things they do.

Obviously, a brain is unnecessary for reproduction, which mussels do quite well when conditions are right. In Maine, they spawn in late spring or early summer after the phytoplankton have "bloomed," or increased in concentration. Following some cue that is not completely understood, the majority of

---

MUSSEL CULTURE in France began by accident. More than 700 years ago, shipwrecked Irishman Patrick Walton planted poles in tidal flats and stretched nets between them to catch seabirds for food. He soon found the mussels growing on them made for good eating, and France is so indebted to this happenstance discovery that a street is named after him: *Rue Patrick Walton.*

mussels in a bed will spawn simultaneously. When the first guy goes (releasing a spawning pheromone), the rest usually follow, filling the water with orange and white clouds. Gametes meet and make microscopic eggs which, in six to twelve hours, develop swimming cilia and become larvae. Within 24 to 48 hours they are already eating baby phytoplankton and growing the larval shell, at which point they are called veligers because they have swimming organs called velums.

In three to four weeks the infant mussel is a quarter of a millimeter long, and when it develops gills and a foot, it is called a pediveliger. It stops swimming and settles to the bottom of the sea or on a suitable surface. When it finds something it likes, it loses its swimming cilia and stays put. At this stage, it may hide out in eelgrass "meadows" for awhile, or settle on filamentous algae. When it sets out its byssus, it is completing its final metamorphosis, but it is by no means immobile. With the help of a drifting byssus thread, which can be up to 200 times longer than the shell, restless mussel "spat" up to 2 mm long can float on the tide en masse, until they settle (more or less) for good. There is a 90 percent mortality rate for juvenile mussels, and those that survive become sexually mature at one to two years of age. They typically live for 12 or 13 years, though some elders make it to the half-century mark.

The two halves of the shell are opened and

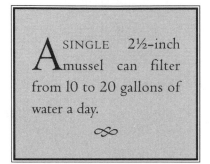

A SINGLE 2½-inch mussel can filter from 10 to 20 gallons of water a day.

∞

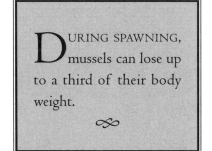

DURING SPAWNING, mussels can lose up to a third of their body weight.

∞

closed by the adductor muscles. The shell's exterior is generally very dark blue or black, and when dry or old it flakes off to reveal the bluish or mother-of-pearl prismatic layer underneath. The "tidal" lines on the shell give only a rough indication of age, but are not accurate. Biologists view lateral sections of shell through the microscope to get the true age.

While the composition of mussel beds is about 90 percent mussels, a variety of other species live in and on the colonies. Kelp use the shells as anchors; barnacles settle in, and shrimp and small fish make feeding excursions to and from the beds. Starfish and green crabs make meals of the mussels, and sea cucumbers and other creatures find mussel neighborhoods to their liking.

Mussels have a smorgasbord of plankton to choose from, as there are around 800 species of them, all highly edible. In spring, diatoms with their rigid silicon skeletons make up the largest percentage of biomass in Maine waters. At other times, ciliates (swimming algae) or dinoflagellates make up the bulk of mussel food. Dinoflagellates are phytoplankton with animal-like characteristics. Like plants, they convert sunlight into chlorophyll, but they also eat other plankton.

A quarter of the food mussels eat is living organisms; the rest is detritus—dead organic matter. A liter of sea water contains 10 to 20 million edible tidbits for mussels to graze on. Maine mussels are tastiest around April because of heavy plankton

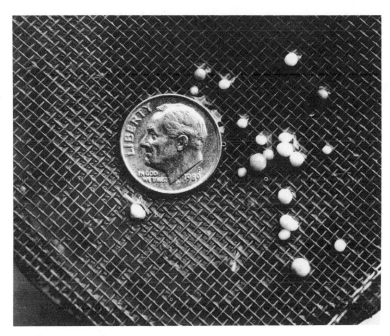

Pearls from mussels vary in size

blooms which make them plump, and high glycogen concentrations which make them sweet.

Due to recent improvements in studying genetic differences of mussels, much of what was once thought to be *Mytilus edulis* has been reclassified as either separate species or as sub-species. *M. edulis* is considered to be the ancestral species from which similar forms evolved. *M. trossulus* is found on the West Coast from California to Alaska, and has been found in Atlantic Canada. It is thinner-shelled, slower-growing, and in Puget Sound it falls prey to disease before it is two years old. *M. californianus* is common along Southern California north to Alaska, and tends to grow in areas exposed to the full force of the ocean. This causes it to grow heavy shells and a tough byssus, and has little commercial significance. The big horse mussel with tougher meats, *Molodious molodious*, is found in deeper, colder waters in the Atlantic, and is also not harvested commercially.

M. edulis, contrary to much existing literature, does not grow on the Pacific Coast, and what was mistaken for it was often *M. galloprovincialis*, the Mediterranean mussel common in Spain. The discovery was a boon to cultivators. The Mediterraneans grow more quickly and have larger meat yields, and are being successfully farmed in suspended cultures in California and Washington state. It is believed that these European mussels colonized the Pacific coast centuries ago from the bottoms or the ballast of Spanish galleons, and some think the Puget Sound hitchhikers may have come from modern globe-hopping vessels docked at the naval shipyard in Bremerton, Washington.

In all, there are 17 species of edible mussels worldwide, most of them cultivated for human consumption. But for poets and artists, the lowly mussel has a symbolic significance.

"Come here, thou proud pretender unto arts,
Most self-amazing sophy, look and learn;
Nor travel more from east to west for food.
Advert thine eye, in contemplation close,
On these thy little betters heaven-fed.
Up to yon luminary raise a thought,
Whose majesty so mild, in all her forms,
The mighty ocean follows faithfully;
View her with wonder leading up the waves
To give unto this mussel due repast.
In full felicity behold it fixed,
Contented waiting the appointed time;

Now sleeping in its cell, wherein anon
'Twill drinking lie at ease, like Romans couched.
Solomon clothed in all his glory (said
The truth itself) was less than lily fair.
O may I modest, and with reverence
To that great oracle, go on to say
His table, on a festival, could not
Exhibit entertainment suited more
To hunger and to health, nor so superb
As Neptune feasts this less than reptile with.

O Fate, thou grand disposer of events,
Director of man's metamorphosis,
Grant me at death a change to mussel-life!
Or, if not too presumptuous in the wish,
More nobly bless me in the oyster-bed!

You furious folk, for fame infatuate,
Who Alexander down your days abrupt
For one long night upon Bellona's* pillow,
Because 'tis curtained round with specious ensigns;
I tell you, fighting fools, this mussel-bed
As much of honor has, and more delight.

Hail, happy shell! from heart-ache ever free!
The basis beautiful of Christendom,
The source of all the potentates on earth,
In its best attitude resembles thee.
Patient, like thee, that prime of nature lies
T'imbibe the quintessence of flowing sweets."

—George Farewell
"There's Life in a Mussel. A Meditation." 1733

---

*Bellona was the Roman goddess of war

Freshwater Mussels

FRESHWATER MUSSELS evolved from their salt-water brethren which were trapped in what became freshwater areas. The United States is home to about one-third of the world's freshwater species of mussels, which are a different kind of animal from the edible blue mussel. Unfortunately, 12 of the 300 native species are considered extinct, and 42 others are federally protected.

Freshwater mussels are not considered edible, but they have been valued (and overharvested) by button-makers and poachers who sell them to the Orient to be used in the cultured pearl industry. The recent invasion of zebra mussels is also taking its toll on native species in numerous rivers and lakes.

Freshwater mussels have a quaint collection of names, among them: shiny pigtoe, pimpleback, birdwing pearly, fine-rayed pigtoe, pocketbook mussel, and rough rabbitsfoot.

Freshwater mussels have quirky family values. In late summer, males release the sperm into the water, where it is siphoned by the females to fertilize their eggs. They retain the developing eggs until the following spring, when the larvae leave home and attach themselves to a host fish so they can disperse. Certain kinds of fish are preferred by each species, and if the fish disappear, so do the mussels. After a three-week ride on the host fish, the little mussels drop off, possibly burying themselves into the river bottom, and aren't seen again until they are three or four years old.

California Mussels

∽

THE CALIFORNIA MUSSEL, *Mytilus californianus*, can buy itself some protection from extremes of heat and cold, but at a price. The red alga seaweed known as *Endocladia muricata* offers shade and insulation to those intertidal mussels that allow its settlement on their shells. Actually, the seaweed anchors onto barnacles already on the mussel shell. But the extra drag that the seaweed generates could cause the mussels to be ripped from their moorings during a storm. Those mollusks that want to go it alone simply wipe the seaweed off their shells with their feet. It's a gamble, and the hardier *M. edulis*—the common blue mussel—does just fine, thank you, without the seaweed.

Zebra Mussels

∽

LIKE SOMETHING from a Stephen King novel, the tiny zebra mussel *Dreissena polymorpha* is invading America. Introduced into the Great Lakes by the emptied ballast of a foreign ship, this prodigious freshwater mollusk from Russia is covering up every nook and cranny of suitable substrate within its reach, and has spread into eight major river systems. By the year 2000 this voracious colonizer will likely be found all over North America.

The striped shells of adult mussels average under an inch to an inch-and-a-half in length, and because there are few predators or natural environmental controls, these mussels are wreaking havoc on the ecosys-

tem as well as to human structures. They gang up on water intake pipes of reservoir pumping stations, power plants, and industrial facilities, blocking the flow. They also cling to boats, dams and piers. Their sharp shells and decaying bodies are affecting recreational beaches on Lake Erie, and the economic impact in the Great Lakes alone could reach $5 billion by the year 2000.

On the plus side, their role in filtering water has caused significant improvements in water quality in some of the affected areas.

Greenshell Mussels

∽

PERNA CANALICULUS, the greenshell mussel, formerly known as the green-lipped mussel, is New Zealand's contribution to the cultivated mussel market. The New Zealand industry has trade-marked the name "greenshell mussel" for it, differentiating it from the wild Thai green mussel which is smaller and not sold fresh in the U.S.

Grown on longlines, these mussels are larger than the blue varieties, and have a lovely green edge to their shells. Half the production of greenshells twenty years ago was ground up into a powder, bottled, and sold in health stores in the U.S. and Europe as a cure for arthritis. In 1982 the U.S. FDA cracked down, saying powdered mussels didn't live up to its claim, and eventually the mollusk was marketed exclusively as a gourmet food.

The greenshell's best market is Japan, followed by the U.S. and Australia.

The 4 major methods of cultivating mussels (from left to right): raft, longline, bottom, bouchot.

CHAPTER FOUR

MUSSEL AQUACULTURE IN NORTH AMERICA AND THE WORLD

THE NATIVE AMERICANS were known to have eaten mussels, and in 1622 the bivalves sustained the Pilgrims. Yet there isn't much else in the American historical literature about mussel consumption until the early 1900s. During World War I, a government campaign to interest people in new sources of protein nearly depleted the Massachusetts mussel beds. Mussel use declined until World War II, when another campaign successfully got people to ease food shortages by consuming the shellfish. But it hasn't been until the last 20 years that North Americans have gotten serious about mussels.

According to the Food and Agriculture Organization of the United Nations, the total world mussel harvest of all edible species in 1992 was 2.7 billion pounds. The United States produces only an infinitesimal fraction of this, and though it is a new industry, it has great significance for those North Americans consuming millions

> T HE ENTIRE world harvest of edible mussels of all species in 1992 was 2.7 billion pounds, live weight.
>
> ∞

of pounds annually. While New England leads the country in mussel harvests, other regions are sustaining viable industries with off-bottom cultivation.

California

C ALIFORNIA'S MOST UNIQUE CULTIVATOR is Ecomar, Inc., growing mussels on a dozen oil platforms three to 12 miles off the coast of Southern California. In the mid 1980s, Bob Meek, a marine biologist, was studying ways to rid oil platforms of unwanted sea creatures when he got the idea to harvest and sell the mussels growing on them "bouchot" (French) style. Oil companies were paying another firm up to $150,000 per rig to blast the unwelcome denizens off, as they eventually fill the six-foot gaps between girders. This increases stress which can destabilize the platforms in strong seas.

After taking years to convince the oil companies they could save loads of money, and persuading the health department that the waters tested safe, Meek was given the go-ahead to cultivate mussels on the platforms. He now sells between 300,000 and 500,000 pounds (shell weight) a year to local chefs and to buyers as far east as Chicago. However, as

oil rigs are removed, other substrates need to be found; Meek is beginning open-ocean longline cultivation of Mediterranean mussels to provide a reliable supply.

Washington State

∞

A LMOST NO MUSSELS are harvested commercially from the wild in Washington state. All commercial activities by the handful of farms involve suspended culture, producing about 2.8 million pounds (shell weight) of the meaty mollusks. However, the native *Mytilus trossulus* succumbs to environmental stress and disease due to the warming influence of the El Niño current, and must be harvested before it is two years old. Wild populations of *M. galloprovincialis*, the Mediterranean mussel, have been discovered recently in Puget Sound and the Pacific Ocean. This has been great news for mussel growers, because the Mediterranean grows much faster and is hardier.

At Taylor United, Inc., mussels from the original broodstock of *M. galloprovincialis* imported from California are bred in a hatchery located in Quilcene. Adult mussels are placed in 10,000 gallon tanks to spawn. They are then removed so they don't eat their young, and the 50 to 100 million free-swimming larvae left behind are fed phytoplankton raised in separate tanks.

When they are ready to metamorphose, they are drained into a mesh net and transferred into smaller settling tanks. Within a week they lose their swimming cilia, attach themselves to the screened bottoms and become sedentary, anchoring themselves with their byssus threads. They are no longer larvae. They are seed. They remain in these tanks between three weeks and two months, depending on the water temperature, then they are removed from the screens and placed on "window screen frames" at the grow-out site in Puget Sound. When they are about a half-inch long, they are scraped from the screens and placed in plastic mesh stockings. Up to a thousand of these nets hang from each of the 40 rafts on various lease sites, and each raft supports 15 tons of mus-

Rafts anchoring socks for suspended mussel culture at Taylor United in Washington state.

sels. They are thinned after a month or two, and these fast-growing mussels are ready for the table after about a year. Production is between 360,000 and a half million pounds, and the company is aiming for five million pounds by the end of the decade.

Seed is moved outside all year long, providing a continual harvest. To keep away the scoters and gold-eneye ducks which also enjoy an easy feast, underwater nets are placed around the rafts.

The largest part of the company's operations is centered around manila clams and oysters. Mussels, which comprise less than ten percent of the company's revenues, were first farmed in 1990-91. Interestingly, these mollusks are at their best when oysters and clams are the weakest after spawn, so the company has prime shellfish to sell year-round.

At Penn Cove Mussels, Inc., off Whidbey Island, *M. trossulus* is grown off rafts, but there is no hatchery involved. Because the geography of the cove in Puget Sound provides a nutrient trap from the outflows of two rivers as well as from the "Olympic rain shadow" which increases sunlight, it is the most prolific natural mussel-settling area in the state.

In early spring, thousands of fibrous rope-like lines about 10 feet long are tied to rafts called "seed lines." When the wild population of mussels is about to spawn, the seed lines are suspended in the cove, usually in April. After spawning, the veliger larvae swim in the warmer surface waters for about three weeks, then they settle on whatever is available, including the seed lines. They are about ¼ millimeter in size when they "set," and are then known as "spat" or "seed."

Thousands of baby mussels collect and grow so quickly that they have to be thinned. In September, the seed lines are pulled from the water and the three-quarter to one-inch mussels are stripped from them and washed into plastic-net socks that are about 20 feet long. Up to 1200 of these socks are resuspended from the raft and the mussels, after reattaching, wangle their way through the mesh so that they are poking out of it. They grow like this until they are harvested a year from their spawning date at 2¼ to 2½ inches long.

If it weren't for shellfish growers in Puget Sound, water quality in the growing areas may have deteriorated due to the tremendous population growth in the region in the last two decades. Because mussel and other shellfish growers depend on clean water, they have fought hard to maintain water standards and to halt pollution. Like canaries in a coal mine, if the shellfish were no longer safe to harvest, then it would also no longer be safe to dig for clams, rake for smelt, swim, fish, or water ski in the cove. In addition, the rafts have created miniature reefs sheltering perch, salmon smolts and shrimp. A thin layer

of mussel shells on the bottom now provides a substrate for anemones, bottom fish, crabs and shrimp. The rafts themselves provide a roosting and feeding spot for seabirds and herons, as well as a safe haul-out spot for otters, harbor seals, and sea lions.

Canada

∞

PRINCE EDWARD ISLAND dominates the Canadian mussel industry, with around 100 growers producing more than 13 million pounds of suspended-culture mussels in 1994. This represents nearly 85 percent of the Canadian mussel production.

The PEI industry began in the mid '70s, and uses the longline system in protected estuaries. The "Italian sock" is used in the province, similar to those used in Washington state. However, instead of being suspended from sturdy rafts, the rope-socks are hung from the longlines, which are 300-foot-long lengths of ½-inch polypropylene rope held near the surface by buoys. Each line holds approximately 120 socks about 6 to 9 feet in length. The seed (½ inch to one inch) is placed in the socks each fall and harvested after 12-18 months. The visible indicators of the farm are the many lines of buoys stretching for acres, and the mussel farmers in their boats dotting the water as they tend their crops.

Unlike the temperate waters of

Longline buoys on a mussel lease site at Prince Edward Island, Canada

Puget Sound, PEI estuaries freeze two to three feet thick in winter. Longlines left at the surface would be destroyed by ice, so prior to winter they must be submerged at least 4½ feet beneath the water surface and at the same time be kept off the bottom so the mussels don't fall prey to starfish or crabs.

Because market demand in PEI is at its peak in winter, a "little" ice doesn't keep the critters off store shelves. Mussel farmers use chain saws equipped with a special ice-cutting blade to make a hole in the ice. A diver goes beneath the ice and ties a rope to the mussel lines and releases them from their moorings. A winch on the ice and an "A" frame are used to haul the lines to the surface. The heavy socks are cut and the mussels transported to shore where they are processed in government-inspected plants and sent on their way. These suspended mussels are known for their plump, grit-free meats, consistent quality, and steady supply.

The Canadian government is encouraging aquaculture development in Newfoundland, Nova Scotia, and New Brunswick following the recent collapse of the groundfishing industry there. One San Francisco distributor imports cultivated mussels from these provinces, and claims the "Newfy" mussels have better flavor because of the cold Labrador current which carries greater nutrients and stimulates glycogen production. In 1994, nearly one million pounds (shell weight) of mussels were cultivated by 30 Newfoundland farmers using longlines.

> THE 1992 per capita total seafood consumption in the U.S. was 15 pounds. Certain regions of France and Belgium have a per capita consumption as high as 20 pounds of just MUSSELS!
>
> ∞

Around the World

∞

NORTH AMERICA is a relative newcomer to this idea of farming seafood. Aquaculture has been practiced in the Far East since at least 500 B.C., and oyster culture was recorded by the early Greeks and Romans. According to the U.S. Department of Agriculture, aquaculture produces about 17 percent of the world's seafood (it was around 10 percent in 1983), and cultivated mussels rank third in production behind carp and brown seaweed.

Approximately 17 species of edible mussels are harvested or cultured worldwide. The blue mussels, *Mytilus edulis* and *M. galloprovincialis*, are the most commonly landed species. China leads the world in total tonnage of mussels harvested, with Spain second, the United States 12th, and Canada ranking 19th.

France began its mussel cultivation by accident 700 years ago when a shipwrecked Irish sailor Patrick Walton strung a net between two poles in the ocean to catch seabirds for dinner. He found that the mussels growing on the poles made a hearty meal, and so the "bouchot" industry was born.

There are now over 700 miles of mussel poles stitching the coast of France. These oak poles are placed in long rows three feet apart in areas where they and their delectible mussels are exposed at low tide. The mussels can be thinned and harvested easily, but grow more slowly because they are not submerged and feeding 'round the clock. Basically family operations, these farms have the lowest meat yield per acre, but France's long expanses of intertidal mudflats make this type of cultivation ideal.

Bottom culture in the Netherlands has existed for more than three centuries. Plots are leased from the government, and wild seed is dredged and replanted to sites 10 to 20 feet deep. Mussels reach marketable size in about 20 months, yielding 15,000 pounds of meat per acre. Most cultivation takes place in the Waddenzee on Holland's northwest coast, and in the Oosterschelde, and beds are protected from the North Sea by encircling islands. Because the mussels are dragged from the muddy bottom, they were formerly deposited on the hard, sandy bottom of the Rhine estuary near the Belgian border to purge themselves. But when these cleansing areas were diked in the mid '80s, the Dutch government developed purging tanks to do the job. Dutch methods have been successfully adapted by Great Eastern Mussel Farms in Maine.

In Spain, culture on hanging ropes began in 1901 at Tarragona on the Mediterranean coast. In the late 1940's the Galacian region, which now comprises the bulk of Spanish mussel production, entered into cultivation of *M. edulis* and *M. galloprovincialis*.

Spain produced more than 200,000 metric tons of *M. galloprovincialis* in 1990. Three-quarters were consumed by Spaniards. Upward of 3500 mussel operations, many family-run, grow the mussels on huge rafts from which ropes are suspended. This vertical use of the water column results in the highest yield of any mussel operation in the world, up to 300,000 pounds of meat per acre.

The average raft has 700 ropes, each 30 feet long. Though rafts are now of modern constuction, they used to be made from old, sturdy wooden boats.

In China, three species are harvested commercially. *Mytilus corucus* is gathered wild off the rocks it grows on and is not farmed. The green mussel *Perna viridis* is cultured, but it is the common blue, *Mytilus edulis*, that is most commonly grown. Large-scale hatcheries for the blue mussel were begun in the early '70s, and seed is grown on lines used for kelp cultivation after the seaweed is harvested. Other farms use longlines.

In Thailand, green mussels, *Perna viridis*, are cultured on bamboo poles or palm stakes driven into muddy bottoms where mussels naturally occur. They are also incidentally cultured on fish traps, where they take up fortuitous residence. The Thai people call them "hoi malong-poo." The striped horse mussel *Musculus senhauseni* (hoi ka-pong) is also harvested, not for people, but for duck farms.

New Zealand has carved itself a niche exporting farmed greenshell mussels, *Perna canaliculus*. Mus-

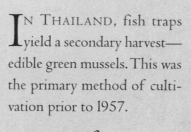

IN THAILAND, fish traps yield a secondary harvest— edible green mussels. This was the primary method of cultivation prior to 1957.

IN THAILAND, mussels are declumped and cleaned by stomping on the netted mollusks while they are underwater.

GREAT EASTERN uses pogy oil made from the pogy (POE-gee) fish to replace hydraulic oil in its dockside processing plant. This organic oil is more environmentally friendly than petroleum-based oil.

∞

MUSSEL SHELLS and culls from Great Eastern's plant are ground and hauled to a family farm in Maine where they are combined with sawdust to make a compost and topsoil additive.

∞

sel culture began there in the late 1960s after this native mussel was overfished by the dredging of wild beds. They are now grown on longlines and reach marketable size in 18 months. Formerly known as green-lipped mussels, because of the lovely tinge along the edges of the shells, their new name was trademarked by New Zealand. Spat is collected in the wild using a specially developed "Christmas tree" rope which obtains a dense settlement. Also, seaweed washing up on the beaches encrusted with mussel seed is air-freighted to the growing areas and attached to the ropes with stockings. Interestingly, the native blue mussel, *Mytilus galloprovincialis*, (formerly thought to be *Mytilus edulis*), has been regarded as a competitor and a pest.

As the world's population increases, so will the need for protein to feed it. Science tells us that each step an animal is higher up the food chain, the more "energy" is lost in the consumption of lower forms. A given amount of plankton eaten directly by humans, for instance, would feed more of us than would the mussels or the big-fish-that-ate-the-little-fish-that-ate-the-plankton. We aren't likely to dish up a plate of algae, but mussels, being closer to the original energy source, are one of the most efficient producers of edible protein and therefore key players in European and Asian diets. The potential for providing mussel protein to a growing world population is enormous, and the challenge will be how to farm the ocean without wounding the ecosystem which sustains it. Mussel expert Sarah Hurlburt writes, "Imagine 43 billion pounds of meat a year from an area of water the size of Cape Cod Bay, which is less than 300 square miles!...This...would provide every living person in the United States with a ton of meat per year. It is technically feasible now."

As wild fisheries become overharvested, the relative stability of aquaculture makes more sense. And the heart-healthy, protein-efficient edible mussel is already one of the most cultivated seafoods in the world.

Eat seafood,
live longer;
Eat oysters,
love longer;
Eat mussels,
last longer.
Anon.

∞

∞

CHAPTER FIVE

STALKING THE WILD MUSSEL

ECAUSE MUSSELS were a subsistence food during hard
times, they still carry with them a certain social stigma. Bob
Lewis of the Maine Department of Marine Resources said,
"When I first moved up here, someone told me that during the
Depression his family used to sneak out and get the mussels after dark
so their neighbors didn't know how poor they were."

Now mussels have come out of the closet, and people of all social
classes take delight in gathering their own bounty from the sea. Foraging
can be a simple procedure, but some precautions need to be observed.

First and most important, be sure your mussels are gathered in an area
that has tested safe from pollution and "red tide." Some beaches are closed
year-round due to sewage runoff or because they are in heavily used harbors;
other beaches are closed only when red tide (a bloom of toxic algae) is
present, or following heavy rains which wash pollutants and organic matter
into the sea. Some areas will also be posted with signs indicating a closure.

Second, assemble your materials. Bring knee boots, tide chart, garden rake or hand trowel, rubber gloves, a bucket, and a cooler with ice.

Third, find your prey. The best mussels will be those that have spent the longest time underwater, so foraging during a moon or drain tide (extreme minus tide) will uncover mussel beds that are exposed only infrequently. In other times, search close to the waterline during low tide.

Remember the motto: "The Shell Can Tell." Old mussels will have thick, rounded, mottled shells with the black protein layer worn off, revealing a dusky blue or silver underneath. They may also have barnacles, which will need to be scrubbed off before cooking. The older the mussel, the greater the likelihood of tooth-breaking pearls. Additionally, large mussels may have a lower meat yield.

The best mussels will also be young ones between two and three inches long with shiny black shells and sharp, pointed edges. You can pry them off either with your bare fingers, or with a garden trowel or a small rake. To test for pearls before you pluck a meal's worth, shuck a few while alive and inspect. Put the knife blade in the small gap where the foot comes out and run it along the outer side of the broad edge, around the adductor muscle. Pearls will be found on the mantle's outer edge.

If your mussels are clumped together, pull them apart. However, if you plan to store them for a few days, don't declump or debeard until the day you use

> "Of the crow-blue mussel shells, one keeps
> adjusting the ash heaps;
> opening and shutting itself like
> an
> injured fan."
>   from "The Fish"
>   Marianne Moore, 1935
>
>   ∞

them. Pulling the byssus threads increases the chance of injury to the mussels.

They may not need to be purged because those growing on rocks probably don't have much sand inside. But to be sure, you may wish to put them in an onion bag and hang them off the side of a boat or dock or buoy in an unpolluted harbor overnight.

Store in a container with a false bottom, such as a double boiler or a cooler with a grate. After putting the mussels in the container, put ice on top. Water, as it melts, drains to the bottom and won't "drown" the critters. If you put them in a refrigerater or walk-in cooler, protect them from direct exposure to dry, blowing air.

When ready to cook, rinse in a colander and scrub off barnacles and other debris with a wire brush. If you're careful to get young, fast-growing ones, you won't have to do much work. Then pull off the beards, pulling from the broad end to the hinged end.

You can cook them right on the beach if you want. In a large pot over the campfire, steam the cleaned mussels in wine or water, or use the Steamed Mussel recipe on page 62.

On a charcoal grill, add a few sticks of hickory or applewood, then set the cleaned mussels on the grill. They will steam in their own juices and pop open in just a few minutes. A shore "Bake" can be had with whatever other sea denizens can be found. Bring some ears of corn and gather seaweed while foraging for the edibles. The most practical method,

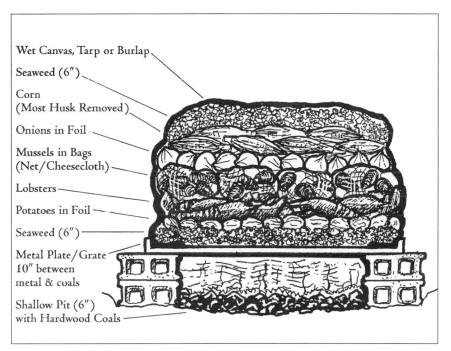

Wet Canvas, Tarp or Burlap

Seaweed (6″)

Corn
(Most Husk Removed)

Onions in Foil

Mussels in Bags
(Net/Cheesecloth)

Lobsters

Potatoes in Foil

Seaweed (6″)

Metal Plate/Grate
10″ between
metal & coals

Shallow Pit (6″)
with Hardwood Coals

A beach bake with lobsters and mussels can be great fun

but the least fun, is to do the Stovetop Lobster Bake on page 98.

The oldest method, used in colonial days, calls for excavating a shallow pit in the sand, lining it with rocks, and burning a hardwood fire on top of the rocks for ten hours or until the rocks are red hot. Usually the fire is started the night before so the fire can build coals. Or it is started at dawn for a late afternoon/early evening feast. First add seaweed or rockweed to the red hot rocks; then add potatoes (in foil), lobster, chicken (optional, in foil), mussels (individual portions in a net bag or cheesecloth sleeve works best,) onions (in foil) and corn (with all but the innermost layer of husk removed.) Cover with damp seaweed and wet burlap or canvas. Keep cover damp and place stones on top to hold it in place. Cook exactly one hour after everything gets hot and

the canvas cover is too hot to touch.

Another method calls for a barbecue-style stone pit built with rocks, bricks or cement blocks to 16 inches high. A large charcoal grill can be used instead. It is best if the coals used are from a hardwood fire allowed to burn three hours down to red hot embers, but charcoal briquettes are an adequate substitute.

Place a solid metal plate covered with aluminum foil 8-10 inches over the fire. It will keep the smoke out and moisture in. A few heavy layers of aluminum foil covering a metal barbecue grate or grill can be used instead. Once the plate gets hot, place a layer of seaweed on the plate first. Then add the ingredients listed above. Cover everything with seaweed. For moisture, sprinkle about a gallon of salt water for each dozen people, or fresh water with three percent salt added. Seal with a canvas or burlap tarp, tucking in the edges on top of the metal plate so they do not burn and the steam is contained. Keep the tarp wet. Cook one hour after everything gets hot, as per previous recipe.

The ambience of eating outdoors and the anticipation built up during the mussel bake ritual seems to create a very healthy appetite. Don't feel guilty about asking for seconds, since shellfish are high in protein and omega-3's, and low in fat, calories and cholesterol.

Precautions

∾

A VERY SMALL PERCENTAGE of people are allergic to shellfish, and should avoid eating mussels. Allergic symptoms usually appear immediately, and include skin eruptions, hives, shortness of breath, tingling of the lips, swelling (particularly in the throat), and digestive disturbances.

However, another problem called shellfish poisoning or "red tide" can affect anyone. Shellfish poisoning has been recorded throughout history, and in most of the world's oceans. Eskimo legends tell of encounters with toxic shellfish, and 18th century Pacific Coast explorers reported illnesses after eating shellfish. Native peoples on both coasts noticed a nighttime bioluminescence they called "sea fire" that was associated with shellfish poisoning, caused by a bloom of toxic algae. Maritime folklore has it that fishermen used to chew up raw mussel meat and hold it against their cheeks for a few minutes. If it caused tingling or numbness, they knew the beds were poisonous.

There are over 10,000 species of phytoplankton (single-celled algae) in the world's oceans. Only a few dozen are known to be toxic, and what falls under the name "red tide" includes diverse toxic species as well as non-toxic algae. The most common red-tide toxin in the United States is called PSP, paralytic shellfish poisoning, caused by a population explosion of microscopic dinoflagellates (phytoplankton with animal-like characteristics.) Poisoning is caused when people eat shellfish which have fed on the algae and have accumulated its toxin.

Mussels accumulate algal toxins more rapidly and to a greater extent than most other commercial bivalves. The good news is, they also detoxify rapidly. Clams, oysters, and whelks are also susceptible to red-tide poisoning, which occurs more frequently on the Pacific Coast than the Atlantic. Lobster, crab and shrimp meats are not affected by red tide.

One thing to remember: shellfish poisoning can be present even though there is no visible "red tide." And not all red tides are caused by toxic organisms. Some are from harmless dinoflagellates or ciliates. For instance, *Mesodinium rubra*, a ciliated protozoon, is common in Maine coastal waters in August and September, and actually provides a healthy meal for clams and mussels.

The federally approved mouse bioassay is the best way to determine the presence of the toxin, and each state monitors for red tide using this test. In Maine, primary sampling stations at the major headlands conduct frequent tests in summer. Liquid from 100 grams of ground-up shellfish meat is extracted and injected into a mouse. Concentrations of toxin are determined by how long it takes the mouse to die or to exhibit reactive behaviors. If toxin levels

> I T WAS ONCE THOUGHT that cooks could detect toxins in shellfish if they put a piece of silver in the water. If the coin turned black, the shellfish was contaminated. Not true, according to "The New Larousse Gastronomique." The coin turns black if mussels are not fresh and give off hydrogen sulfide.
>
> ∾

are 80 micrograms (one microgram is one millionth of a gram) per 100 grams of shellfish, secondary sampling stations in estuaries and bays are activated and closures are effected. This is far below the level known to cause human illness. Maine's red-tide season is generally from June until October.

There are different types of shellfish poisoning:

PSP—paralytic shellfish poisoning—*Alexandrium tamarense*. This is the only shellfish poisoning found in Maine. Symptoms: tingling and numbness of lips, mouth and fingertips; general muscular weakness, numbness and respiratory distress. Symptoms can begin almost immediately, and if noticed you should call the poison control center or a hospital emergency room for treatment.

DSP—diarrhetic shellfish poisoning from the *Dinophysis* species. Occurs in Europe.

ASP—amnesiac shellfish poisoning (domoic acid toxin from the diatom *Pseudonitzschia pungens*). This is a new toxin which first appeared in Prince Edward Island, Canada in 1987. This organism is a common member of the phytoplankton community and has not been previously known to produce toxins, nor has it caused poisoning in mussels in the United States. It is detected with a High Performance Liquid Chromotography (HPLC) assay.

NSP—neurotoxic shellfish poisoning—from the *Ptychodiscus brevis* (formerly *Gymnodinium breve*) organism. It is found in Florida and warm waters where mussels are not found, and appeared for the first time in North Carolina in 1987, carried from Florida by current systems associated with the Gulf Stream.

Since the Maine Department of Marine Resources began monitoring the coast in the 1950's, there have been no deaths or serious illness in Maine from red tide in legally harvested mussel beds. The only problems have been when shellfish were illegally harvested in closed areas. A study of over 500 water samples at Great Eastern's mussel growing areas from 1987—1991 revealed no blooms of toxic phytoplankton.

Those foraging for a meal from the wild would be wise to observe all precautions regarding closed beaches. Because of constant testing, shellfish purchased from harvesters fishing in certified waters are the safest of all.

CHAPTER SIX

PURCHASING, HANDLING AND PREPARATION TIPS

HERE'S NOTHING MORE DISAPPOINTING than cooking up a fish fillet that looked pretty in the grocer's case, but tastes like recycled cardboard when on your plate. Because of the inconsistent quality of seafood and the "horror stories" of seafood illnesses, consumer confidence in seafoods is not what it could be. However, you can increase your chances of bringing home a quality product if you arm yourself with a little information and aren't afraid to ask questions.

Unfortunately, sometimes the people behind the seafood counter don't have the answers. We once visited a retail store in the Midwest. Incognito, we asked the person behind the counter what those blackish shellfish in the two-pound bags were.

"Those are mussels," replied the young fellow. "They grow in freshwater swamps. People go out into the shallow water and harvest the mussels with their toes grasping the shells." Needless to say, this was shockingly inaccurate, albeit amusing. We later found out he was from Nicaragua where freshwater mussels may be harvested as he described!

Each shipment of mussels is given a lot number, which traces it to the bed and the date of harvest.

The most important thing you can do is to purchase your seafood from a reputable dealer or market, and also to check for a certified shellfish-shipper's number on the package or by asking the counter person. For example, Great Eastern's number ME 309SS is on every package, giving the assurance that the shellfish are harvested from state-approved beds.

Because mussels are a new offering in some markets, special care is taken to educate the people who sell them to you. We send monthly newsletters to supermarket merchandisers and handling tips to fish markets stressing the importance of maintaining the shelf life of mussels by keeping them on ice. Mussels are living animals. The warmer their environment, the higher their metabolism, and the quicker they will die. Sometimes GEM's careful instructions are ignored by busy merchandisers. That is why it is up to you to know how to buy the best mussels.

For instance, mussels should not be displayed in live lobster tanks or in shellfish display tanks.

Mussels, being active filter feeders, produce more ammonia than these systems can handle, tainting themselves with the flavor. Also, wet tanks are generally at a higher temperature than is good for the mussels, causing them to spoil quicker.

Make sure packaged mussels are not over-wrapped at the store, or they will suffocate. Great Eastern pioneered the use of two-pound plastic retail bags to sell mussels. These bags, which retain moisture, have holes that allow excess water to drain and the mussels to breathe. Closing the bag is a tag with a "use by" date and the lot number—important pieces of consumer protection.

Occasionally consumers are wrongly told that they can freeze their mussels. Don't you believe it. Never, EVER freeze live mussels. They should only be frozen after they are cooked. Take the meats out of the shells and freeze with a little of the broth. These are ideal for chowders. In the wild, mussels in intertidal areas are often subjected to freezing in the winter. However, a clear hemolymph acts as an antifreeze, protecting them at low tide when they ice up. They are able to thaw when the tide returns, lifting the ice cap above the beds and bathing them in "warm"(er...29 degrees or so) nutrient-filled water to rejuvenate. If you accidentally freeze yours, there is no hope of revival, and if you cook them they will be of poor quality and have a stringy meat texture.

Wild, unpurged mussels are often sold in bulk, or shipped in onion bags. Many are taken from crowded beds where the mussels take six or seven years to reach market size—the age at which tooth-breaking pearls are common. Due to abrasion from tides and currents, they will have lost some of their outer black protein layer and will often appear to be colored blue and silver, particularly at their hinges. Since most wild mussels are not purged in rewatering tanks, they can be sandy or gritty tasting. They may cost less per pound, but could command a high price in consumer dissatisfaction.

Cultivated mussels, or those from prime quality wild beds, have thin, light, jet-black shells. They may be "small" but have larger meat yields and are free of detectable pearls. Those with apricot-colored meats are the girls, and the white meats are the boys. In spring, mussels may have "black sacks," due to feeding on abundant green algae. This makes them extra tasty, and because of the glycogen they build up prior to spawning, they will be fat and sweet.

Mussel shelf life after packing at the plant is from 9 to 14 days, depending on the season. They will remain happy and content in the fridge as long as you do your part. Stand the bag up in a bowl. Put a half dozen ice cubes in the top of the bag and close it up. You can put ice cubes on the bottom, too, but you have to make sure the mussels never sit in water. Mussels left in fresh water quickly use up their oxygen and suffocate. Never place in an air-tight container, and don't soak them before cooking. They don't need to be treated like clams in this regard.

Most of our recipes call for steaming the mussels, and here is the proper way to do it. First, inspect your mussels, throwing out ones with broken shells. If there are any with opened shells (gapers), run them under cold water or give them a firm thwack with your fingers. If they close even a little, they are alive and can be eaten. It is not necessary for the critters to snap tightly shut. Just as long as they move.

If they don't move at all, they may either be dead or playing hard to get. Pack them in ice, or place in the freezer for a FEW minutes. Or be more aggressive with your thwacking and see if that doesn't help. Sometimes you can see movement in the fleshy interior, indicating a mildly perturbed but very much alive mollusk. Gaping is the mussel's way of breathing out of water, especially if it warms up or dries out. It is a sign of stress, and it is trying to breathe. Mussels kept on ice in the fridge will have fewer gapers than those simply shoved into the meat compartment, because they need a moist, cool environment in which to breathe.

To store in fridge, stand the bag of mussels up in a bowl. Put a half dozen ice cubes in the bag and close up. Drain water as it accumulates.

Those with shells gaping widely or which move from side to side are suspect and should be tossed, along with *any* that have an off-odor. Living mussels have the sweet smell of the sea, hinting at the tempting meal you are about to have.

Extra-heavy mussels that are closed may be full of mud. The last thing you want is one of these unloading its cargo in your kettle of broth. Toss it, too. Usually a "mudder" can be discovered simply by squeezing the shells and sliding them apart from each other.

After you have your mussels in the cleaning pot, run them under cold water and take the beards off. Rope-cultivated mussels tend to have heavier beards of which they produce more to keep themselves anchored on the ropes. However, many are de-bearded prior to sale. Bottom-harvested mollusks in areas of low currents and crowded neighborhoods tend to have less byssus. If you buy Great Eastern mussels, they usually won't have much byssus at all, because during their 24-hour-plus layover in the tanks at Long Cove, they are discarding these beards. They have sensed the lack of tension on them, so they cast them off in anticipation of growing new ones. This process begins right in the tanks, the mussels sending out fine filaments up to three inches long which attach to each other and to the sides of the tank. It even continues in the bags, which is why you may see thin pale webs sprouting from the mussels, ending in a spot of glue on some neighboring bivalve.

The beards, in case you hadn't figured it out, are little bundles of dark steel woolish fibers protruding from between the mussel's shells. (One fellow from Albany, NY called our hotline number and said his mussels were swallowing hairballs! While keeping a straight face, we assured him it was beards he was seeing, and that it was his job to yank them off. That seemed to satisfy him and he hung up, presumably to cook his first batch of hairball-free mussels.)

The hairballs...er, beards, are attached to the mussel's foot, and when they are yanked off, they cause damage to the innards, which is why they should NEVER EVER be pulled off until just before you are going to cook them.

Most folk simply pull from the broad end to the narrow end where the shell is hinged, and that takes care of that. Some people may prefer to snip them with scissors or a knife, but yanking probably gets most of the beard out. They are now ready to cook.

To steam your mussels, you can use either water, wine or beer. If the recipe includes using broth, it will be specific. If

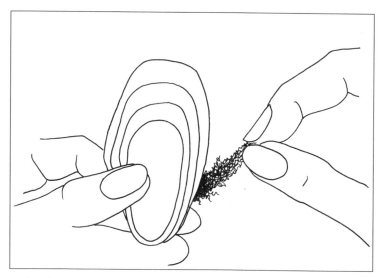

Debearding a mussel just before cooking—pull from the broad end to the narrow end for the best results.

you are steaming the mussels as a preliminary to some other use (such as baking), it's your choice. Usually a half-inch in the bottom of the pan will steam them up nicely.

Pour the liquid in the pan, set the mussels in, then cover with a tight-fitting lid and turn on high. Shake the pot a few times as the lid begins to rumble, to evenly distribute the heat. In four to five minutes the shells will pop open and the meats will ball up and pull away from the shell. If they are stringy or "stuck" to the sides of the shell, they aren't fully cooked. The Dutch fishermen like to let the lid rattle three times at a full boil, shaking the pan each time, to guarantee doneness.

Leftover cooked meats can be preserved with the addition of Italian salad dressing (oil and vinegar) and chopped vegetables, making a marinated mussel salad. It will stay fresh for up to seven days covered in the fridge. Shucked meats and salads can also be purchased at supermarket deli sections. Mussel meats are commonly used for smoked mussels, chowder, in marinara sauce over pasta, as a seafood pizza topping, wrapped in bacon and broiled or barbecued, or deep-fried in clam batter.

Mussels can be used in any recipe that calls for clams. Use 12 mussels per person for appetizers and 25-30 per person for a main course. A two-pound bag will serve two as an entrée, or four as appetizers or as a main meal with rice or pasta.

If the recipe calls for shucking the mussels, that simply means taking the meats out of the shell after steaming. You can save some of the shells to use as garnish, or if you are adventurous, do as the Dutch do and use them as tongs to eat the other mussels with.

You can also create marvelous crafts with them.

After your meal, rinse the shells and set them outside. There is a little organic matter left on them, and you don't want the house to smell. (Although you *could*

Christmas garland of mussel shells made by Great Eastern employee Charlene MacDonald and her daughter.

smash them up and use them in the garden compost; they are a good source of calcium and nitrogen.) After awhile, assuming they haven't been carted away by some critter, they will be bereft of odor and ready to use in wreaths, Christmas ornaments, flower arrangements, key chains, you name it. (This might be a good way to entice the kids to eat their mussels.)

Then again, Maine cookbook author Leslie Land says, "Food preferences are among the most deeply ingrained of learned behaviors; some members of famine-threatened populations have starved rather than accept unfamiliar nourishment." Go figure.

In short, there are those who feel the best way to eat mussels is steamed in wine and herbs. Nothing more. But for those who like a little variety, we have searched the countryside for recipes that will inspire new culinary delights. So go ahead. Eat your mussels.

LIST OF RECIPES

∞

Quick-to-fix

ENTRÉES

* Belgian-Style Mussels (Belgium), 84

Mussels with Linguini and Perfect Spaghetti Sauce (Italy), 85

* Easy Linguini and Clam Sauce with Mussels, 86

Mussel Jambalaya (Cajun- U.S.), 87

Paella (Spain), 88

Mussel Risotto (Spain), 89

New England Mussels in a Vermouth /Saffron Sauce (New England), 90

Cape Cod Tarragon Fried Mussels (New England), 91

Cozze Mona Lisa (Italy), 92

* Salsa-Steamed Mussels (Mexico), 93

* Mussels in Blue Cheese Sauce (Belgium), 94

Seafood Fra Diavolo (Italy), 95

Mussels with Shiitake Mushrooms (Regional U.S.), 96

Mussel Moussaka (Greece), 97

Maine StoveTop Lobster Bake (New England), 98

Latitudes Mussel Maderia (New England), 99

Stir-fry Mussels (Thailand), 100

Lebanon's Bowl of Rice, 101

Mussel Putanesca with Pizza Sauce, 102

* Delicious Desperation, 103

SALADS

Summer Dream Sea Salad (Regional U.S.), 105

Mediterranean Mussel & Pasta Salad (Italy), 106

* Yucatan Mussel Salad (Mexico), 107

* Easy Mussel Salad in Avocado (Regional U.S.), 108

* Cold English Mussel Salad (England), 108

BRUNCH

Mel's Mussel Frittata (Regional U.S.), 109

Mussel Quiche (France), 110

* Curried Mussels On English Muffin (Regional U.S.), 111

Mussel Crêpes (France), 112

CHAPTER SEVEN

NATIONAL RECIPE CONTEST
Top Three Winners

IN 1993, Great Eastern sponsored a national recipe contest, which was advertised in *Simply Seafood Magazine*. Fifty recipes were submitted to be judged on three categories—taste, originality, and history. The stories behind the recipes ranged from fictional flights of fantasy to family histories such as, "My grandfather came from Italy and cooked this every Sunday..."

A committee of Great Eastern staff judged the recipes based on a score from one to ten in each of the three categories. A panel of chefs then judged the top ten recipes, narrowing them down to four. A cook-off was held at the East Wind Inn in Tenants Harbor, and chef Shane Ward prepared the top four recipes to be taste-tested by fourteen of GEM's staff and family members. The results were factored into the judges' scores and the winners were announced.

"The Best Damn Mussels You'll Ever Eat" lived up to its billing, receiving a "ten" in all three categories. Chef Ward stated, "The simplicity of the recipe coupled with the wonderful flavors of jalapeño and rosemary, not to mention the story, makes this my number one choice." The recipe garnered Washington state residents Cathy Silvey and Richard Wood a three-day windjammer sailing trip on the coast of Maine.

The rest of the recipes have come from various sources. Not only did we include many of the recipes entered in the contest, we gathered recipes from mid-coast Maine chefs, friends, and Great Eastern staff to provide a sampler of mussel dishes for nearly any palate.

Our next cookbook? Mussel Desserts. (Just kidding.)

BEST DAMN MUSSELS YOU'LL EVER EAT

A REGIONAL U.S. RECIPE BY CATHY SILVEY AND RICHARD WOOD
MERCER ISLAND, WASHINGTON
Winner of First Place in GEM National Recipe Contest

THE ORIGINAL NAME of the recipe described, but did not evoke, the true essence of the dish—"Mussels with Jalapeños, Rosemary, and Cheese on Pasta."

We had been accepted as cook-off finalists at the West Coast Oyster Shucking Championship and Washington State Seafood Festival in Shelton, Washington. We knew we hadn't taken the event seriously enough when at 4:00 A.M. we frantically tried to pack utensils, pots, ingredients, and place-settings for the five judges into an old cooler. Our suspicions were confirmed when we arrived at the festival to discover that the cooking events were held on-stage in front of a live, large, and very demanding audience. The situation became more ominous as we watched the first contestant.

She was dressed in a black, low-cut evening gown, and as she leaned forward to begin preparation we overheard one of the judges gasp, "Look at the mussels on that dish." The second chef was a master craftsman at presentation—a statue, marble place settings, white gloves and tails. We looked at our tie-dyed tee shirts and mismatched table settings and concluded that we had a very good chance of making complete fools of ourselves.

We were scheduled to cook at 1:00 P.M., and by 11:00 had become so discouraged that we wandered off to look at some of the other events, thinking maybe we'd just hop in the car and go home.

But first we had to try some oysters wrapped in bacon, with a glass of Chardonnay. And then oysters on the half-shell and some micro-brew. And then a Cajun oyster sandwich and some more micro-brew. And then some smoked salmon and more Chardonnay.

About 12:45 we found ourselves back at the cooking event, but for some reason things didn't look so terrifying. Maria, a woman from the Philippines, was finishing up a seafood salad. Gene, the master of ceremonies, was grinning. "We are running a little behind schedule, folks!" he proclaimed. And looking at us and two other contestants, asked if we wouldn't mind preparing our dishes together on-stage to save time.

We retrieved our old cooler and realized we had forgotten a strainer for the pasta. We retrieved our blanc de blanc. Timothy, the be-tailed chef of the morning was getting ready to fix a second dish. "Gene's been into the white wine, too," he said, passing over a bottle and filling two glasses for us. "I never cook without wine."

Suddenly things seemed a whole lot better. We moved onstage to de-beard and clean the mussels. Another contestant was arguing with Gene. "I DO NOT COOK with ANYONE ELSE onstage!" Gene smiled and said, "Well, today you do." We asked if we could use the sink. She glowered and shrieked, "I CAN'T TALK WHILE I'M COOKING!" And she began to open three cans of Campbell's Cream of Mushroom soup for her crab casserole.

So we peeled the garlic and chopped the jalapeños, and had some blanc de blanc, and grated the cheese, and started the pasta water, and smelled the aroma of mushroom soup, and offered Timothy some blanc de blanc. Then it was our turn.

The actual cooking is kind of hazy. We did remember to wash our hands first, but we completely forgot to taste anything. Our mismatched settings looked kind of cute in front of the judges. We presented our dish and as we watched the judges sniff and poke and sniff some more, we anxiously waited for one of them to taste the food. Finally they started to eat. The wiry little Italian judge took a bite, his eyes lit up, he turned to the woman next to him and exclaimed, "THESE ARE THE BEST DAMN MUSSELS YOU'LL EVER EAT!"

Well, we didn't win first prize. That went to Maria and her seafood salad. But the judges did seem to think that this mussel recipe was the best in the main dish category.

1⅓ lbs. fresh angel-hair pasta
2 Tbsp. olive oil
2 Tbsp. unsalted butter
3 cloves garlic, minced
½ cup onion, minced
2 medium jalapeño peppers, de-seeded and finely chopped (use seeds if you're adventurous)
2 tsp. fresh rosemary leaves

1 cup Chardonnay
2 lbs. mussels
½ cup heavy cream
1 cup jack or Swiss cheese, grated and tossed in a bag with 1 Tbsp. flour to coat

OPTIONAL: Garnish with fresh oregano (chopped) and Parmesan cheese

Serves: 4

Cook angel hair pasta. Drain, then toss with olive oil. Put pasta in large serving dish and keep warm.

In large pot, sauté garlic, onions, jalapeños, and rosemary with the butter for one minute. Add wine and mussels. Turn heat to high and steam for 3 minutes until shells open. Remove mussels with slotted spoon and arrange in shells over pasta. Keep warm.

To the broth in the pot, add cheese and cream, then simmer until sauce starts to thicken, stirring occasionally. Remove from heat and pour over mussels and pasta.

Garnish, then serve with crusty French bread and salad.

WINE RECOMMENDATION: Cream, cheese and pasta suggest a rich barrel-aged Chardonnay which complements the "creaminess" in the dish.

PER SERVING: 13 oz. (360 g.)/ Calories 883/ Total fat 39 g./Sat. Fat 13 g./ Cholesterol 280 mg./ Sodium 486 mg./ Carbohydrate 89 g./ Protein 34 g.

Low Sodium

THE LAST MANGO IN COUPEVILLE

A REGIONAL U.S. RECIPE BY CATHY SILVEY AND RICHARD WOOD
MERCER ISLAND, WASHINGTON
Winner of Second Place in GEM National Recipe Contest

THIS RECIPE WAS SERVED at the Captain Whidbey Inn as a finalist during the 1993 Mussel Festival in Coupeville, Washington. What follows is the account of how the recipe was developed.

It was in the late '30s, just before the outbreak of World War II. We were living in the South of France, near Marseille, and running a small Italian restaurant. A friend of ours, Abdul Shawaib from the West of Africa, imported produce from his native country and delivered fresh fruit and vegetables to the restaurant every day or so. He also had a contract with the free French army, which at that time was barricaded under heavy seige behind the walls of Paris. Abdul Shawaib had an old black Cadillac and he would make the trip from Marseille to Paris on nights when the moon was new and he had his ways of running the blockade. The fresh produce greatly increased the will of the Resistance to continue its struggle, and the Germans intensified their patrols on the nights when it was rumored that Abdul Shawaib was on the road.

As the Germans increased their pressure, Abdul Shawaib devised new and more devious means to outwit them. His final ploy was to cover his produce, which filled the back seat of the Cadillac, with a tarp and then spread a layer of mussels just thick enough to hide the cargo. Mussels then did not have the reputation as the delicacy they enjoy today. In fact, the French would feed them to their dogs and cats and draft animals.

On his last run, under the cover of mussels, Abdul Shawaib loaded a shipment of mangos in the old car and in the gathering dusk set off up the autobahn. It was close to dawn when he sighted the bonfires atop the walls of Paris. He stopped at the rendezvous but was surprised by a German patrol which forced him outside the car. The young German lieutenant, who could not have been more than eighteen, strutted to the window and poked at the mussels with his swagger stick.

"And what, pray tell my good fellow, is this?" he inquired of Abdul Shawaib. Our friend, whose mind was racing, reached under the tarp and exclaimed, "Alas, mangos in the Coupe de Ville!" He drew forth a piece of the succulent fruit, and as the officer leaned forward to sniff, he squished it into the German's face and sharply rapped him across the back of the head. As the soldier slumped forward, the patrol exploded in panic. Shots were fired, the Cadillac raked by automatic weapons fire. Abdul Shawaib was seriously wounded but managed to escape in the confusion. Slowly he made his way back to Marseille, hiding the huge car in haystacks during the day. A man on the run, he begged us to take him and hide him, so we gave him a job as cook in our restaurant.

And what a cook! Somehow the events outside Paris melded in his mind, and he created his most famous of all recipes, which combined the mussels and mangos. But Abdul Shawaib never told us the recipe, nor did he divulge its name. It was simply known to our patrons as THE RECIPE. In retrospect, we really believe that the rejuvenating properties of this dish are greatly exaggerated. Of course, the people who ate it lived longer, but they didn't actually become younger. In any event, it was the restaurant, not our customers, that was short-lived.

The gathering fires of war were flamed by the unholy alliance forged between the Germans and Italians. Hoards of ethno-centrifugal Italians streamed west out of Italy, burning and pillaging. Our humble restaurant became a victim to this cultural-purification campaign. We were on the rocks the day it happened, fishing for ice squid. Abdul Shawaib was alone in the kitchen. We found him on the floor, his mind and body almost gone. His last word harkened back to the episode outside Paris. "WHAT IS THE RECIPE?" we shrieked over the onslaught of his coming demise. But all he heard was the German, and all we heard was "The Last Mango in Coupeville."

How we found Coupeville is another story. And so is how we derived the secret of the RECIPE from the reconstituted DNA of our departed friend. We were totally amazed at the secret ingredient.

---

3 cloves garlic, chopped
¼ medium onion, chopped
2 Tbsp. fresh ginger, chopped
2 Tbsp. olive oil
½ red bell pepper, chopped
1 cup white wine
2 lbs. mussels
1 cup jack cheese, grated

2 Tbsp. flour
½ cup cream
⅔ lb. fresh linguine or angel-hair pasta to serve two
⅓ cup pine nuts, roasted
2 tsp. fresh rosemary, chopped
1 large mango, chopped

In 6-quart cooking pot, sauté garlic, onion and ginger in 1 tablespoon olive oil over medium heat until onions are translucent. Add red pepper and cook another minute. Add wine and mussels. Cover and steam until mussels just begin to open. Coat cheese with flour (shake together in bag) and add to mussel pot along with the cream. Stir well and continue to cook covered until the mussels are all open.

Cook pasta in boiling water until done. Drain. In large serving dish, toss pasta with 1 tablespoon olive oil, pine nuts, and rosemary. Top with mussels. Garnish with mango.

Serves 2

WINE RECOMMENDATION: Cream and ginger are great matches to a rich "creamy" Chardonnay.

PER SERVING: 26 oz. (725 g.)/ Calories 1527/ Total fat 70 g./ Sat. fat 17 g./ Cholesterol 341 mg/ Sodium 742 mg./ Carbohydrate 159 g./ Protein 61 g.

Low Sodium

BUTTE FALLS MUSSELS AND MORELS

A REGIONAL U.S. RECIPE BY CHUCK HANCOCK
BOISE, IDAHO
Winner of Third Place in GEM National Recipe Contest

BUTTE FALLS IS A TINY TOWN tucked in the Oregon Cascades. My wife and I spent a wonderful dozen years there working for the Forest Service. While we loved every moment, we often missed the coast. I suppose that's what happens to transplanted New Englanders who have a drop of salt water in their veins.

In New England, eating mussels was always a tasty way to round out a day spent with a couple of friends and a six-pack while introducing seaworms to striped bass. All one needed was a mussel shoal, a small driftwood fire, and a few empties with beer for steaming.

The first time I ate farmed mussels, we were in Maine as the guests of Mait and Peg Griggs. The Griggs introduced us to a friend (Ed Myers of Abandoned Farms) who put on a mussel feast that evening. We bought these mussels from a fairly new (two years comes to mind) farmer who had been a professor at Princeton. The feast was superb and I have never passed by an opportunity to sample farmed mussels in any restaurant when they come around on the menu.

The event stuck in my mind for twenty years now, because as this gentleman reduced my ignorance of mussels, I noted he had a certain look in his eye. It was a look of contentment with perhaps a touch of bemused surprise that everyone hadn't figured out the secret of life.

I didn't understand that look until years later when I moved out west to a town of 400 and began working for the Forest Service. Several years later a visitor from back East remarked that I had a certain hard-to-define look that he didn't recall being there before.

Once or twice a summer we'd head for the Oregon Coast to feast on seafood and long walks. Coming home we'd bring a slew of wild mussels in a cooler of seawater. Because I was a forest worker, wild morels were no stranger to our table. Since both mussels and morels have an affinity for buttery wine sauces, this recipe was inevitable.

2   lbs. mussels
1½   sticks butter (6 oz.)
4   cloves garlic, chopped fine
4   Tbsp. chopped parsley (or fresh
      chervil)

1½   oz. dried or 12 oz. fresh morels
      (reconstitute dried morels in wine)
1   cup white wine
      salt and pepper to taste

You will need a piece of mushroom for each shell—about 50 mussels. 12 oz. fresh shitake or oyster mushrooms can be substituted.

Resist the temptation to add other seasonings. There are two flavors starring in this dish: the mussels and the morels. All the sauce needs to do is to build a bridge between them, not cover them with a blanket.

Steam mussels until just open but short of done (they'll finish under the broiler later.) Melt butter and over a gentle heat sauté the garlic and parsley. Add the morels and wine. Raise the heat to medium and sauté until done, about five minutes. Remove the morels and reserve. Raise heat to medium high and reduce the wine without burning the butter. When you reach a desired thickness, stop cooking. If you want a glossy sheen, thicken with cornstarch.

To assemble, remove the mussel meats and spread the shells flat. Put the meats into the sauce to coat and place each back on one half of the shell. Place one piece of morel on the other shell.

Broil the mussel/morels only until the mussels are just done—not an instant more. Serve with cups of sauce for dipping.

Serves 6 as appetizer

WINE RECOMMENDATION: This buttery dish needs the contrast of a crisp, clean Chardonnay with little or no oak aging. An herbal Sauvignon Blanc would also be a nice accompaniment.

PER SERVING: 4 oz. (112 g.)/ Calories 289/ Total fat 24 g./ Sat. fat 14 g./ Cholesterol 81 mg./ Sodium 333 mg/ Carbohydrate 8 g./ Protein 6 g.

CHAPTER EIGHT

Appetizers

Mussels are bite-sized, quick to cook,
and come in their own single-serving "dish"—their shell.

These can also be served as entrées. Generally an appetizer recipe
will serve two per pound of mussels, or one as a main dish.

DIJON STEAMED MUSSELS

FRANCE

Quick to fix

2 lbs. mussels	¼ cup onion, chopped
juice of ½ lemon	¼ cup Dijon mustard
3 cloves garlic, minced	⅓ cup heavy cream
1 Tbsp. butter	pepper
¼ cup white wine	parsley for garnish
2 Tbsp. olive oil	⅔ lb. fresh linguine

Steam mussels with lemon juice, 1 clove garlic, butter and wine for 4 minutes. Remove from pan and keep warm, reserving broth.

Sauté in oil over medium heat 2 cloves garlic and onions until tender, about 3-4 minutes. Add Dijon mustard and cream; simmer 3 more minutes. Season to taste with a little broth and pepper.

Arrange mussels around individual bowls of linguine. Pour cream sauce over pasta and mussels; garnish with parsley.

Serves 4

WINE RECOMMENDATION: The great white wine of Burgundy, where the village of Dijon is located, is Chardonnay. This rich dish would go well with a creamy, barrel-aged version.

PER SERVING: 7.4 oz. (207 g.)/ Calories 475/ Total fat 23 g./ Sat. fat 8 g./ Cholesterol 148 mg./ Sodium 619 mg./ Carbohydrate 48 g./ Protein 18 g.

GARLIC is more potent when it is crushed than when it is minced. An enzyme is set loose when the garlic cells are broken, reacting with the garlic oil to form a chemical that gives the distinctive (and highly odoriferous) scent.

Mussels with Escargot Butter
France

Shortly after immigrating from Scotland in 1973, my wife and I found escargots both difficult to buy and expensive in Chicago. When mussels first appeared on the market, we decided to try them with escargot butter—which doesn't need escargots to prepare. We've been eating them ever since. (We use double garlic and sleep back-to-back!)

Geoff. Davies, Miami Lakes, FL

3 oz. unsalted butter
3 cloves garlic, finely chopped
4 spring onions or scallions, finely chopped
½ tsp. tarragon, dried
1 Tbsp. fresh parsley, chopped
1 Tbsp. olive oil
several pinches turmeric
2 lbs. mussels

Four hours before preparing the dish, soften butter, then mix thoroughly with garlic, onions, tarragon, parsley, olive oil, and turmeric. Return to refrigerator to harden.

Steam mussels in water or white wine. When opened, discard half of each shell. Arrange mussels in shell in single layer on ovenproof plates.

Preheat oven to 350 degrees. Place dab of flavored butter on each mussel. Place in oven for 3-5 minutes until butter is melted and heavenly garlic smell emerges.

Serve with warm French bread to dip in broth.

Serves 4 as appetizer or 2 as main course

Wine Recommendation: A crisp Fumé or Sauvignon Blanc to pick up the herbal notes in the dish would be a wonderful wine here.

Per serving: 3 oz. (82 g.)/ Calories 236/ Total fat 22g./ Sat. fat 11 g./ Cholesterol 74 mg./ Sodium 319 mg./ Carbohydrate 3 g./ Protein 8 g.

MUSSEL MOZZARELLA

ITALY

Contributed by Mel Pell, New York, New York
Great Eastern corporate chef in the 1980s

This can be prepared in advance and held warm in a chafing dish.

2 lbs. mussels
2 Tbsp. olive oil
2 Tbsp. chopped fresh parsley
2 Tbsp. chopped chives
2 cloves garlic, finely minced

dash red pepper (cayenne)
freshly ground black pepper
12 oz. mozzarella cheese, shredded
lemon wedges
rock salt

Steam mussels in water or wine until open. Discard top shell and drain bottom shells with meat.

Pre-heat broiler to 450 degrees.

Sauté parsley, chives, garlic and peppers in olive oil for 2-3 minutes. Mix in bowl with mozzarella cheese.

Spread small jelly-roll pan or 9 x 13 inch pan with rock salt on bottom.

Spoon cheese-herb mixture on each mussel to fill shell, and pat down evenly.

Place mussels on rock salt (to prevent them from rolling over). Broil until golden brown and bubbly.

With any extra topping, spread on French bread and broil along with mussels until toasted.

Serve 3-4 mussels per person with lemon wedges

WINE RECOMMENDATION: The rich cheese flavors here need a balance from a crisp, non-oaked Chardonnay or dry Chenin Blanc.

PER SERVING: 5.2 oz. (146 g.)/ Calories 326/ Total fat 21g./ Sat. fat 10 g./ Cholesterol 76 mg./ Sodium 539 mg./ Carbohydrate 5 g./ Protein 28g.

MUSSELS IN TOMATO AND PARMESAN CRUST

ITALY

Extra-Lean ∽ Low-Fat

THE BEEF INDUSTRY created "Real Food for Real People," and the Pork Industry created "Pork, the Other White Meat." However, for many years the seafood industry has been fragmented in its marketing and promotion. Then, in the late 1980s, with money generated from taxes on foreign fish imports, the Seafood Promotion Council was created. Their television ads featured the Official Spokesfish telling consumers to "Eat Fish and Seafood Twice a Week." The following recipe was part of a media campaign generated by the Council and sent out to food writers. Their goal was to promote the variety of seafood and the many ways it can be prepared at home.

4 lbs. mussels	⅛ tsp. cayenne pepper (or to taste)
¼ cup dry white wine	2 Tbsp. freshly chopped tarragon leaves
¼ cup water	(2 tsp. dried)
reserved mussel broth	2 Tbsp. fresh lemon juice
20-oz. can Italian plum tomatoes,	salt and pepper to taste
drained and finely chopped	¼ cup Parmesan cheese
2 large cloves garlic, finely minced	¼ cup bread crumbs

Place mussels, wine and water in 4-6 quart pot over high heat. Cover and steam mussels until just open, 3-5 minutes, shaking pan occasionally to cook evenly. Remove mussels from pan, retaining liquid.

Working over reserved broth to catch additional liquid, remove and discard one shell of each mussel. Place mussels on baking sheet filled with dried beans, rock salt, or crumpled foil to hold mussels in place. Cover while preparing sauce.

Combine mussel broth, tomatoes, garlic, cayenne pepper, tarragon and lemon juice in saucepan over medium-high heat. Cook and stir mixture until reduced and thickened, about 10 minutes. Add salt and pepper to taste. While sauce reduces, mix together Parmesan cheese and bread crumbs.

Spoon tomato mixture over each mussel. Sprinkle with cheese mixture. Broil in preheated broiler just until topping is golden and crusty, about 2 minutes.

Serves 4-6

WINE RECOMMENDATION: A young, non-tannic red wine such as Pinot Noir, Merlot or an Italian Chianti would be terrific.

PER SERVING: 6.8 oz. (192 g.)/ Calories 120/ Total fat 3 g./ Sat. fat 1 g./ Cholesterol 40 mg/ Sodium 479 mg./ Carbohydrate 8 g./ Protein 12 g.

MUSSEL BROCHETTE

ITALY

A BROCHETTE IS A SMALL SPIT or skewer which is used to broil or roast meat, fish, or vegetables.

2 lbs. mussels
¼ cup white wine

¾ pound sliced bacon
maple syrup (optional)

Steam mussels in wine and remove meats. Discard broth and shells, or save some shells for garnish.

Cut bacon strips into thirds. Par-cook bacon in microwave or pan until fat turns clear and pliable, but NOT crisp. Allow to cool enough to handle comfortably.

Wrap each mussel meat with a strip of bacon. If meats are small, use two meats inside each bacon strip. Put 6-8 wrapped meats on skewer. Broil or barbeque, rotating once, with high flame until bacon crisps. Drizzle with maple syrup if desired.

Serves 6-8 as appetizers; 2 on skewers over rice as entrée

WINE RECOMMENDATION: An off-dry white wine such as Riesling or Gewurztraminer or a soft red wine (served chilled) like Gamay would be a good choice.

PER SERVING: 2 oz. (59g)/ Calories 136/ Total fat 9 g./ Sat. fat 3 g./ Cholesterol 33 mg./ Sodium 368 mg./ Carbohydrate 1 g./ Protein 10 g

MIDIA DOLMA
(STUFFED MUSSEL DELIGHT)
ARMENIA
Low Sodium ∞ Extra-Lean

AS A CHILD brought up in a household of Armenian background, one of my favorite treats for company was an appetizer called Midia Dolma, or Stuffed Mussels. In the original Armenian method, the mussels are left in their shells, and the rice mixture is stuffed into each partially opened shell, and tightly closed by tying with string. They are layered in a pot with water added (no wine) to cook. This always seemed like too much work, and too time-consuming, so I devised my own easy version, with some variations in ingredients. And you don't have to be Armenian to like it.

Mrs. Ankin G. Bertelsen, Fort Lee, NJ

2 lbs. mussels	mussel broth
½ cup white wine	⅓ cup currants
2 Tbsp. olive oil	½ tsp. cinnamon
1 cup chopped onion	salt and pepper to taste
½ cup uncooked rice	2 Tbsp. chopped fresh parsley
¼ cup chopped pine nuts	sliced lemon for garnish
1 cup unsalted chicken broth	

Steam mussels in ½ cup wine, covered, until shells open. Remove from heat and let cool. Strain and reserve broth. In separate saucepan, heat olive oil and sauté onion until tender. Add rice and pine nuts and sauté 3 to 5 minutes. Stir in chicken broth, reserved mussel broth, and remaining ingredients (except parsley). Cover and simmer for 35 minutes or until rice is tender but still firm. Blend in chopped parsley. Spoon onto half shells and chill. Garnish with lemon wedges.

Serves 4-6

WINE RECOMMENDATION: A full-flavored Chardonnay or Pinot Blanc would be a good choice.

PER SERVING: 5.5 oz. (155 g.)/ Calories 205/ Total fat 8 g./ Sat. fat 1 g./ Cholesterol 19 mg./ Sodium 100 mg./ Carbohydrate 23 g./ Protein 8 g.

MAINE COCKTAIL MUSSELS
REGIONAL U.S.
Quick-to-Fix ∞ *Extra-Lean* ∞ *Low-Fat*

Contributed by Mel Pell, New York, NY
Great Eastern corporate chef, 1980s

2 lbs. mussels, steamed, removed from
   shell, and chilled

COCKTAIL SAUCE:
   2 cups tomato catsup
   4 Tbsp. horseradish
   4 Tbsp. Worcestershire sauce
      Juice of two lemons

Combine sauce ingredients and chill. Serve with mussels on hors d'oeuvre plate.

Can also be served in half shell over a bed of lettuce with sauce served on top.

Serves 4

WINE RECOMMENDATION: We'd recommend a soft white wine such as Chenin Blanc or Riesling; a blush White Zinfandel would also work.

PER SERVING: 8.3 oz. (231 g.)/ Calories 211/ Total fat 2 g./ Sat. fat 0/ Cholesterol 28 mg./ Sodium 2073 mg./ Carbohydrate 44 g./ Protein 10 g.

BARBECUED MUSSELS WITH SPICY DIP

Low Sodium ✤ *Quick-to-Fix* ✤ *Extra-Lean* ✤ *Low-Fat*

2 lbs. mussels
1 12-oz. jar prepared salsa, taco sauce, or
   hot pepper sauce

**Charcoal grill with top to cover
(Webber or Coleman style)**

Place mussels on grill in one even layer, about 4 inches above medium hot coals. Cover the grill and cook for 5 minutes. To avoid overcooking, remove mussels from heat when shells are open and the meat pulls away from the shell. Discard any which do not open. Place the mussels in a large bowl and serve with sauce on the side for dipping.

Serves 4 as an appetizer

WINE RECOMMENDATIONS: If the dip has a lot of hot pepper taste, then go with an off-dry (slightly-sweet) wine such as Gewurztraminer or White Zinfandel.

PER SERVING: 9.6 oz. (269 g.)/ Calories 143/ Total fat 6 g./ Sat. Fat 1 g./ Cholesterol 99 mg./ Sodium 177 mg/ Carbohydrate 11 g./ Protein 12 g.

MUSSELS STEAMED ON THE GRILL

U.S.

Quick-to-Fix ✤ *Extra-Lean* ✤ *Low-Fat*

2 lbs. mussels
6-8 Tbsp. white wine

1 tsp. thyme

For each appetizer serving, place 8 to 12 mussels on a rectangle of heavy-duty foil. Shape foil to hold liquid and add 1 Tbsp. white wine and ⅛ tsp. thyme to each packet. Seal and place on grill about 5 minutes, or until shells open. Each packet makes 1 appetizer serving.

Serves 6 as appetizer

WINE RECOMMENDATION: This simple dish would go well with almost any chilled white or blush wine.

PER SERVING: 1.7 oz. (48 g.)/ Calories 42/ Total fat 1 g./ Sat. fat 0/ Cholesterol 19 mg. / Sodium 95 mg./ Carbohydrate 1 g./ Protein 5 g.

MUSSELS STEAMED IN BEER
U.S.
Low Sodium ∞ *Quick-to-Fix* ∞ *Extra-Lean*

THIS RECIPE WAS DEVELOPED for the 1992 International Boston Seafood Show by our consulting chef, Kerry Altiero, of Café Miranda in Rockland, Maine. Because mussels are not as well known in the South as they are in the Northeast, we wanted to have a mussel recipe prepared in a familiar mid-Atlantic/Southern style. Since shrimp boiled in beer and Old Bay is common to this region, we believed that mussels might become more popular if prepared this way.

2	Tbsp. olive oil
½	cup celery
1	cup red onion, medium dice
1	tsp. minced garlic

1	12 oz. bottle of beer
1	tsp. Old Bay seasoning
2	lbs. mussels
2	Tbsp. parsley, chopped fine

In a large pot, sauté celery, onion and garlic in oil. Add beer, Old Bay, and mussels, tossing at least once for even cooking. Mussels are done when all the shells open. Sprinkle with parsley. Serve in bowls with broth and crusty French bread.

Serves 2 as an entrée or 4 as an appetizer

WINE RECOMMENDATION: First choice of course would be a good local ale, followed by a crisp, clean (non-oaked) Chardonnay.

PER SERVING: 14.2 oz. (400 g.)/ Calories 297/ Total Fat 16 g./ Sat. Fat 2 g. / Cholesterol 99 mg/ Sodium 327 mg./ Carbohydrate 17g./ Protein 13 g.

MUSSELS STEAMED IN WINE
(MOULES MARINIERE)
FRANCE
Low Sodium ∞ *Quick-to-Fix* ∞ *Extra-Lean*

THIS IS OUR VERSION of Moules Mariniere—Mussels Sailor's Style. It is one of the most common preparations for mussels, and is what one might get if ordering a steamed mussel appetizer at a restaurant. We have used this recipe at our supermarket cooking demonstrations since 1980. Our retail package has this recipe printed on the back.

2 Tbsp. olive oil
¼ cup chopped onions
2 cloves garlic, finely chopped
¼ cup celery or green pepper
2 lbs. mussels
¼ cup white wine

OPTIONAL GARNISHES:
grated lemon peel
fresh chopped parsley
bay leaf

Sauté onion, garlic, celery/green pepper in oil in a large saucepan over medium heat for 30 seconds. Add mussels and wine. Cook for about 4 minutes, until mussels open. Shake pot occasionally while cooking.

Serve in soup plates with broth, garnished with lemon peel/parsley. Add crusty bread for dipping. Serves 4 to 6 as an appetizer, 2 to 3 as a main course.

ITALIAN STYLE: Add 1 or 2 cups fresh chopped or canned tomatoes, drained, while mussels cook.

Serves 4

WINE RECOMMENDATION: The green pepper and optional garnishes suggest a nice Sauvignon /Fumé Blanc from California or a crisp Italian white such as Orviero.

ITALIAN STYLE, PER SERVING: 6.3 oz. (177 g.)/ Calories 144/ Total fat 6 g./ Sat. fat 1 g./ Cholesterol 99 mg./ Sodium 17 mg./ Carbohydrate 12 g./ Protein 11 g.

THAI-STYLE RED CURRIED MUSSELS
THAILAND
Low Sodium

SINCE THERE ARE 17 SPECIES of saltwater mussels which grow worldwide, mussels have been an important part of the world's cuisines. We picked six recipes from around the world to highlight the international impact of this shellfish and presented them at the International Boston Seafood Show. This is our consulting chef's interpretation of a Thai Curry-Style Mussel dish, and is often on the menu at Café Miranda in Rockland, Maine.

½ tsp. vegetable oil
1 Tbsp. red curry paste
1 Tbsp. fresh ginger, finely chopped
1 can unsweetened coconut milk
2 tsp. sugar

1 Tbsp. plus one tsp. fresh lime juice
2 lbs. mussels
1 bunch scallions, medium chopped
   (1 cup steamed rice per person if
   using as an entree)

In a large saucepan, sauté curry paste and ginger in oil for 2 minutes over high heat, being careful not to burn. Add coconut milk, sugar, and lime juice. Bring to a boil. Add mussels and cover. Steam for 4 minutes or until shells open.

Place mussels in warm serving dish, pour sauce over, and garnish with scallions.

Serves 2 as an entrée with rice, or 4 as an appetizer

WINE RECOMMENDATION: This spicy dish goes well with an off-dry, low-alcohol chilled wine such as Gewurztraminer.

PER SERVING: 20.6 oz (578 g.)/ Calories 738/ Total Fat 45 g./ Sat. Fat 37 g./ Cholesterol 99 mg./ Sodium 30 mg./ Carbohydrate 71 g./ Protein 20 g.

BIG DON'S ZESTY STEAMED MUSSELS
U.S.

Quick-to-Fix

Contributed by Karen J. Carlson, Cranford, NJ

1 small onion, finely chopped

3 Tbsp. small green pepper, finely chopped

2 Tbsp. olive oil

6 large cloves fresh garlic, finely chopped

½ cups water

½ cups tomato sauce

1½ tsp. fresh lemon juice

8 drops Tabasco sauce (more if desired)

2 lbs. mussels

Sauté onion and green pepper in oil until soft. Add garlic and continue to sauté, being careful not to burn. Add water, tomato sauce, lemon juice and Tabasco and simmer for 15 minutes. Add mussels and bring to boil, steaming until shells open.

Serve with garlic bread to dip in sauce.

Serves 4

WINE RECOMMENDATION: A crisp Chardonnay would stand up well to this flavorful dish.

PER SERVING: 5.1 oz. (142 g.)/ Calories 131/ Total fat 8 g./ Sat. fat 1 g./ Cholesterol 28 mg./ Sodium 285 mg./ Carbohydrate 7 g./ Protein 8 g.

MUSSEL AND CRABMEAT FRITTERS

U.S.

Contributed by Mel Pell, New York, NY
Great Eastern corporate chef, 1980s

FRITTER BATTER:

1 cup flour, sifted
½ tsp. salt
⅔ cup milk
2 eggs
1 Tbsp. melted butter

BREADING

2 lbs. mussels
¾ cup fine bread crumbs
½ cup freshly cooked, chopped crabmeat
(can use frozen)
Pinch of salt, pepper, nutmeg
3 Tbsp. olive oil
Lemon quarters
Parsley

Combine all fritter-batter ingredients and blend well.

Steam mussels and shuck.

Mix bread crumbs and crabmeat thoroughly. Season with salt, pepper and nutmeg to taste.

Dip mussel meats in fritter batter, then roll in bread crumb mixture. Sauté breaded meats in olive oil until lightly browned.

Serve immediately with lemon quarters and parsley.

Cocktail sauce works well as a dip for this dish.

Serves 4

WINE RECOMMENDATION: Try a nice dry, sparkling wine from California or Spain.

PER SERVING: 6.6 oz./ (184 g.)/ Calories 406/ Total fat 21 g./ Sat. fat 6 g./ Cholesterol 271 mg./ Sodium 665 mg./ Carbohydrate 30 g./ Protein 21 g.

PLEASANT COVE HORS D'OEUVRES
NEW ENGLAND

Contributed by Mel Pell, New York, NY
Great Eastern's corporate chef, 1980s

2 lbs. mussels
1 lemon, sliced
1 onion, quartered
2 cloves garlic, minced or puréed
1 bay leaf

2 Tbsp. salted butter
1 cup sliced fresh mushrooms
½ cup pitted black olives, sliced
1 Tbsp. parsley
   salt and pepper to taste

Steam mussels in a large pot, adding lemon, onion, garlic, and bay leaf to steaming pan. When done, remove and discard one shell from each mussel. Put mussels in remaining shells in shallow baking pans.

Preheat broiler to 450 degrees.

Melt butter in frying pan. Add mushrooms and sauté until liquid has mostly disappeared. Add olives and parsley; sauté until lightly browned, seasoning with salt and pepper. Put a little of this mixture on top of each mussel, filling shell.

Broil about 5 inches below preheated broiler for about 6 minutes until topping is bubbly and mussels are hot.

Serves 4

WINE RECOMMENDATION: Olives, garlic and mushrooms add an earthy taste that marries well with lighter non-tannic reds such as California Pinot Noir or Gamay, an Italian Chianti or Spanish Rioja.

PER SERVING: 3.4 oz. (95g)/ Calories 137/ Total fat 11 g./ Sat. fat 2 g./ Cholesterol 35 mg./ Sodium 309 mg./ Carbohydrate 4 g./ Protein 8 g.

MUSSELS AU GRATIN

FRANCE

THIS RECIPE was sent to us by the National Fisheries Institute, which is the industry's trade organization. It was featured in a press kit to promote October National Seafood Month.

½ cup water
4 cloves garlic, minced
¾ tsp. pepper
4 lbs. mussels
3 Tbsp. olive oil
¼ cup finely chopped onion

½ cup finely chopped parsley
2 Tbsp. lemon juice
1 cup cracker crumbs
½ cup grated Parmesan cheese
　 Lemon wedges for garnish

In large pot, combine water, half of garlic and pepper. Bring to boil, add mussels and steam on medium until they open, about 5 minutes. With slotted spoon, transfer mussels from broth on to 2 rimmed baking sheets. Break off and discard top halves of shells and any unopened shells.

Heat olive oil in medium skillet. Sauté remaining garlic and onion until soft. Add parsley and lemon juice. Combine with cracker crumbs and Parmesan cheese and sprinkle over mussels. Bake at 400 degrees F. about 5 minutes or until crumbs are lightly brown. Serve warm with lemon wedges.

Serves 4-6 as entrée; 8 as appetizer

WINE RECOMMENDATION: The lemony-parsley flavors here would go well with a rich barrel-aged Sauvignon Blanc.

PER SERVING: 4.2 oz. (118 g.)/ Calories 177; Total fat 8 g., Sat. fat 2 g./ Cholesterol 33 mg./ Sodium 261 mg./ Carbohydrate 15 g./ Protein 11 g.

CHAPTER NINE

SOUPS AND STEWS

Lindsay's Leek and Mushroom Mussel Chowder

Regional U.S.

Low Sodium ∞ *Quick-to-Fix*

Contributed by the corporate offices of Shaw's Supermarkets, E. Bridgewater, MA

4 lbs. mussels, cooked and shucked to
    yield 1 lb. meats
1 oz. olive oil
2 med. leeks, sliced
6 med. fresh mushrooms, sliced
½ cup dry white wine

2 cups milk
1 cup heavy cream
  salt
  pepper
  dash cayenne pepper
  dash paprika

Cut mussel meats in half and set aside.

Cook leeks and mushrooms in oil in 3-quart saucepan on medium high until soft.

Add mussel meats and wine, reduce heat to medium, and simmer 5 minutes. Remove leeks, mushrooms and mussel meats from pan with slotted spoon and set aside. Bring remaining juice in pan to boil; add milk and cream and season to taste with salt, pepper and cayenne.

Bring back to boil, reduce heat, and return leeks, mushrooms and mussel meats to pan. Stir lightly and serve immediately with a dash of paprika.

Serves 6

WINE RECOMMENDATION: A rich "creamy" Chardonnay would be a nice choice here.

PER SERVING: 9.3 oz. (259 g.)/ Calories 332 / Total Fat 24 g./ Sat. fat 11 g. / Cholesterol 102 mg./ Sodium 342 mg./ Carbohydrate 13g./ Protein 14 g.

NEW ENGLAND MUSSEL CHOWDER

NEW ENGLAND

Low Sodium ∞ *Quick-to-Fix*

THIS IS THE TRADITIONAL RECIPE for New England Clam Chowder. We have substituted mussel meats for shucked clams.

2 lbs. mussels
2 oz. salt pork, diced
1 large onion
1 Tbsp. flour

½ cups reserved mussel broth
2 medium potatoes
2 cups warmed light cream
pepper to taste

Steam mussels in large pot with one cup water until opened—about 4 minutes. Remove meats and chop in half. Reserve 1½ cups strained mussel broth.

Sauté salt pork in pot until partially rendered into liquid, about 10-12 minutes.

Add onions and sauté until transparent. Add flour and blend. Add reserved broth, stir, and bring to boil. Add potatoes. Boil until done, about 10 min. Add mussel meats and cream. Stir and season to taste. Remove any salt pork before serving.

Serves 4

WINE RECOMMENDATION: A crisp, clean Chardonnay from California or a French Chablis could all work well.

PER SERVING: 9 oz. (252 g.)/ Calories 530/ Total fat 50 g./ Sat. fat 23 g./ Cholesterol 182 mg./ Sodium 219 mg./ Carbohydrate 12 g./ Protein 10 g.

CREAM OF MUSSEL (BILLI-BI) SOUP
FRANCE

BILLI-BI SOUP is a signature dish of Maxim's in Paris, France. Mel Pell, Great Eastern's first cooking demonstrator, developed quite a number of mussel recipes for the company and this is Mel's interpretation of this well known dish.

1 cup chopped onions	2 cups milk
¼ cup chopped shallots	2 egg yolks
2 Tbsp. (½ stick butter)	1 cup heavy cream
1½ cups dry white wine	½ tsp. salt
4 sprigs parsley, minced	freshly ground black pepper to taste
4 lbs. mussels	1 Tbsp. chopped parsley

In a heavy soup pot, combine onions, shallots, butter, wine and parsley. Place mussels on this bed, cover tightly, bring liquid to boil and steam for 5-7 minutes, or until mussels have opened. With slotted spoon, scoop mussels from pot and set aside. Strain broth through cheesecloth into a bowl. Press down on vegetables to extract all the juices.

Shuck the mussels, discarding any unopened ones. Reserve 24 and purée the rest, along with the strained broth, in blender or food processor. Pour the purée into the top part of a double boiler and set it over hot water. Add milk and heat to scalding. In a small bowl, beat egg yolks with the cream, then, stirring constantly, add a few tablespoons of hot mussel mixture. Stir egg yolk mixture into soup and continue stirring constantly, until the soup has thickened slightly. Season with salt and pepper. Remove soup from heat and serve in individual bowls, adding 3 of the reserved mussels to each portion and garnish with minced parsley.

NOTE: To serve as a cold soup, place pan over cold water to cool it quickly. Then refrigerate. Thin with a little light cream before serving, if necessary. Garnish as for the hot soup.

Serves 6

WINE RECOMMENDATION: This rich dish works well contrasted with a crisp, lemony Sauvignon Blanc or dry Chenin Blanc from California— or a crisp Italian white such as Orvieto or Pinot Grigio.

PER SERVING: 10.5 oz. (293 g.)/ Calories 360/ Total fat 25 g./ Sat. fat 14g./ Cholesterol 155 mg./ Sodium 472 mg./ Carbohydrate 11 g./ Protein 15 g.

SAFFRON MUSSEL SOUP

I ENCOUNTERED THIS AS A SPECIAL at Chez Grandmère on M Street in Georgetown, Washington, D.C. When the chef left—after I had only had it twice—I wept. The entire restaurant has since changed hands. I have no idea where the chef went. I mourn.

Geoff. Davies, Miami Lakes, Florida

½ pint whipping cream
½ tsp. saffron threads
2 lbs. mussels
1 tsp. dried dill
½ stick (4 Tbsp.) salted butter

½ medium onion, finely chopped
2 cloves garlic, crushed
½ pint fish stock or mussel broth
    (can use bottled clam juice)
    white pepper

1 hour ahead of time:

Bring cream to boil, add saffron, then remove from stove. Let steep; cream will take on saffron color and flavor.

Steam mussels with dill. Remove meat from shells.

Melt butter in 2-quart saucepan and sauté onions. Add garlic and continue cooking for two minutes. Add fish stock or mussel broth and saffron cream. Bring to boil and simmer for 3-5 minutes. Add pepper and mussels. Heat thoroughly, stirring constantly. Add water if too thick. Serve with crisp rolls.

Serves 4

WINE RECOMMENDATION: Saffron, dill and cream all seem to suggest a rich Chardonnay with some oak barrel-aging on it.

PER SERVING: 7 oz. (196 g.)/ Calories 356/ Total fat 34 g./ Sat. fat 16/ Cholesterol 119 mg./ Sodium 399 mg./ Carbohydrate 5 g./ Protein 9 g.

FISH MONGER'S STEW

ITALY

This is Chef Kerry Altiero's interpretation of Zuppa de Pesce or a Provençale-style fish stew/soup. (Provençale refers to French country cooking)

Café Miranda, Rockland, ME

¼ cup olive oil

½ lb. hot or mild sausages, sliced ½ inch thick (optional)

5 whole cloves garlic, peeled

2 anchovy fillets, minced

1 red onion, medium dice

1 bulb fresh fennel, julienned

1 28-oz. can peeled tomato, squished (use your hands)

1 28-oz. can crushed tomato

6 oz. heavy cream

½ lb. fish fillet cut into one-ounce pieces

½ lb. medium shrimp in the shell

2 lbs. mussels

6 fresh basil leaves

salt and pepper to taste

balsamic vinegar (for the table)

Brown sausages in oil in saucepan on medium high heat. Add garlic and sauté until golden. Add anchovy and onion and sauté until golden to brown. Add fennel and stir, sauté another minute. Add tomatoes and cream, bring to boil, and simmer for five minutes. (This part can be done up to 3 days ahead and kept refrigerated.)

Add all seafood and increase heat. Steam until mussels pop open. Remove from heat, adjust seasonings, and add basil and salt and pepper to taste. Ladle into a huge bowl and accompany with balsamic vinegar, pepper, and crusty bread at the table.

Serves 4

WINE RECOMMENDATION: This rich tomato-based stew would match well with a flavorful, non-tannic red wine such as a fruity Zinfandel from California or a Chianti from Italy.

PER SERVING: 26 oz. (729 g.)/ Calories 722/ Total fat 48 g./ Sat. fat 17g./ Cholesterol 226 mg./ Sodium 2025 mg./ Carbohydrate 31 g./ Protein 41 g.

TONY'S BARRUDA

PORTUGAL

Extra-Lean ∞ Low-Fat

WHEN SEVERAL OF US at Great Eastern visited Nordic Fisheries in 1988, we had occasion to visit one of the finest fish markets in the Northeast: Benkovitz's located on "The Strip"—Pittsburgh's meat- and produce-packing section.

Among many prepared seafood dishes and seafood salads for sale was a colorful seafood stew that was labeled "Barruda." It looked so good we asked the in-store chef Tony Gratter to give us the recipe. When the Maine shrimp and scallop seasons start in December, we often cook this at home using fresh Maine sea scallops instead of bay scallops. The brown Maine mahogany quahogs are substituted for the traditional white littlenecks.

Compliments Tony Gratter, Pittsburgh, PA

6	green peppers, julienned
2	stalks celery, sliced
2	large onions, sliced thin
1	tsp. garlic, minced
⅓	cup vegetable oil
2	cups white wine
2	lbs. mussels
24	littleneck clams, washed

2	lbs. small shrimp (60-70), peeled and deveined
6	cloves garlic, whole
1	Tbsp. thyme
1½	Tbsp. oregano
1	Tbsp. basil
1	lb. bay scallops
3	28-oz. cans crushed tomatoes

Sauté vegetables with 1 teaspoon garlic and ⅓ cup vegetable oil. Add wine as onions become transparent. Bring back to simmer, then add cleaned mussels, clams, and shrimp. Cover pot, let steam 3-4 minutes. When shellfish are open, add seasonings and bay scallops. Mix in crushed tomatoes and let simmer an additional 3-4 minutes. Serve hot over rice or noodles.

WINE RECOMMENDATION: The "green" herbal notes in this dish would be complemented by a rich herbal Sauvignon Blanc.

PER SERVING: 25 oz. (696 g.)/ Calories 434/ Total fat 11 g./ Sat. fat 1 g./ Cholesterol 187 mg./ Sodium 1585 mg./ Carbohydrate 32 g./ Protein 43 g.

Serves 6-8

PORTUGUESE MUSSEL STEW

PORTUGAL

Extra-Lean ∞ *Low-Fat*

THIS RECIPE is one I created while proprietor/chef of the Madd Apple Café in Portland, Maine. It was a favorite dish and may be considered an aphrodisiac since one evening I got a call for reservations from a gentleman who wanted to know if the Portuguese Mussel Stew would be on the menu. I told him that I would be happy to arrange that. On Saturday evening a young couple came into the café and took the requested "tiny table in the corner." That table was the setting, as it turned out, for the big question—"Will you marry me?" It seems they had ordered the stew on their first date just five months earlier at the Madd Apple Café.

Rebecca Riley, Yarmouth, Maine
P.S. We hope you fall "Maddly" in love with it.

2 Tbsp. olive oil
1 Tbsp. chopped garlic
1 28-oz. can plum tomatoes
3 Tbsp. chopped fresh basil
   pinch crushed hot red pepper

12 small new potatoes, boiled til soft
1 lb. Linguica or Chourico (spicy) sausage, in ¼ inch slices (Polish sausage can be substituted)
4 lbs. mussels

Heat oil in large pot. Gently sauté garlic, add tomatoes, juice and all. Stir in basil and pepper. Simmer 20 minutes. Add potatoes and sausage slices—heat through. Add mussels. Cover and steam until shells open. Serve in bowls with crusty bread.

Serves 6

WINE RECOMMENDATION: Tomatoes and spicy sausage are a great match to a spicy red California Zinfandel.

PER SERVING: 19 oz. (536 g.)/ Calories 449/ Total fat 17 g./ Sat. fat 6 g./ Cholesterol 143 mg./ Sodium 854 mg./ Carbohydrate 48 g./ Protein 28 g.

"FRIENDSHIP" MUSSEL STEW

U.S.—MAINE

Quick-to-Fix

A FEW YEARS BACK, my wife and I were visiting my 93-year-old great aunt living along the coast of Friendship, Maine. Aunt Bertha had minimal provisions in the larder to feed us. As we strolled out to the rocky point exposed by the outgoing tide, we spotted the mussels and filled our shirt tails. Once back in the kitchen, and noting the wine and sherry in the cabinet, we improvised. Butter and a bottle of fresh milk from the dairy down the road (with rich cream at the top) welcomed us from the ice box. Using chopped onions instead of shallots and wishing for parsley, we put together this stew and relished the fresh sweetness of the mussels with the richness of the cream and sherry. A meal and an adventure I'll long remember.

Alden Booth, co-owner People's Pint Brew Pub, Greenfield, Massachusetts

2	lbs. mussels
½	cup dry to semi-dry white wine
1	cup fresh light cream
½	cup fresh whole milk
4	Tbsp. butter

⅓	cup finely diced shallots
½	cup cream sherry
¼	cup chopped parsley
	white pepper
	salt

Steam mussels in wine until opened. In small saucepan, combine cream and milk over low heat. In another saucepan, sauté shallots in butter until soft (3 to 5 minutes). Turn heat to low and add sherry. While stirring, add heated milk and cream mixture and continue to heat slowly. Do not allow mixture to boil.

Remove meats from cooled mussels. Add meats and parsley to cream mixture; heat thoroughly. Season to taste with salt and white pepper. Serve with chowder crackers and crusty bread.

Serves 2 as main course or 4 as appetizer.

WINE RECOMMENDATION: A Riesling or Chenin Blanc with just a touch of residual sweetness would match well with the sweet, woody flavors that sherry imparts.

PER SERVING: 16.5 oz. (463 g.)/ Calories 832/ Total fat 64 g./ Sat. fat 39 g./ Cholesterol 259 mg./ Sodium 1135 mg./ Carbohydrate 20 g./ Protein 20 g.

BOUILLABAISSE

FRANCE

Low Sodium ∽ *Extra-Lean* ∽ *Low-Fat*

A BOUILLABAISSE (boo'-ya-base) is a highly seasoned stew made of several kinds of fish and shellfish.

Recipe courtesy Chef Anita Storch, Craignair Inn, Spruce Head, Maine

STOCK:

1	Tbsp. olive oil
½	cup diced onion
4	julienned leeks (white tender part only)
5	cloves garlic, minced
1	28-oz. can whole tomatoes with liquid
	pinch of saffron/several threads
	(or substitute turmeric)
2	crushed bay leaves
	juice of one orange
3	Tbsp. tomato paste
½	tsp. celery seed

⅓ cup chopped fresh parsley
salt and pepper to taste

SEAFOOD IN THE SHELL:

4	lbs. mussels
4	lbs. (about 40) littleneck or manilla clams
2 or 3	1¼ lb. parboiled lobsters (quarter tail, chop claws) (or substitute similar amount of crab or shrimp in the shell)

Heat oil in stock pot, add onion, leeks, garlic, tomatoes. Sauté until translucent. Add saffron/turmeric, bay leaves, orange juice, tomato paste, celery seed, and parsley. Sauté 10 minutes. Add seafood and water to cover (about 4 cups), and salt and pepper to taste. Simmer 15 minutes until mussels and clam shells open. Serve with garlic bread.

Serves 6

WINE RECOMMENDATION: A fresh, young red wine without a lot of tannin or oak, such as Gamay, would be terrific.

PER SERVING: 9 oz (254 g.)/ Calories 206/ Total fat 5 g./ Sat. fat 1 g./ Cholesterol 128 mg./ Sodium 171 mg./ Carbohydrate 16 g./ Protein 23 g.

CIOPPINO

ITALY

Low Sodium ∾ *Extra-Lean* ∾ *Low-Fat*

AS THE PONDS AND LAKES BEGIN TO FREEZE around mid-December, the first snows arrive on Maine's coast. The season also brings the small Maine shrimp—sold out of small trucks along coastal Route 1—and the Maine sea scallops. This is the best time of year to make cioppino since the mussels have fattened up and are the sweetest. Cusk or hake are inexpensive and always available at this time of year, hake being particularly firm and good for a seafood stew.

2 lbs. mussels
3 cups water
1 Tbsp. olive oil
2 carrot sticks, peeled and diced
2 celery stalks, diced
2 large green peppers, diced
6 large cloves garlic, finely chopped
2 large onions, diced
2 16-oz. cans whole tomatoes, chopped, with liquid
1½ cups mussel broth

1 tsp. basil
2 bay leaves
1 tsp. oregano or coriander seed
2 cups white wine
2 lbs. fresh, firm white fish fillets cut into chunks (cusk, haddock, hake, halibut, monkfish)
½ lb. sea scallops
½ lb. shrimp, shelled and deveined salt and pepper to taste

In large saucepan, steam mussels in 3 cups of water until shells open. Remove and set aside. Reduce mussel broth in half by heating over medium heat, yielding 1½ cups.

In large stewpot, sauté carrots, celery, peppers, garlic, and onions in oil for 3 to 5 minutes until tender. Add tomatoes, tomato liquid, mussel broth, basil, bay leaves, and oregano/coriander. Simmer for 20 minutes. Add 2 cups wine and bring to a boil. Add fish chunks, scallops and shrimp, simmer 5 minutes. Add reserved mussels and salt and pepper to taste. Serve with Italian bread.

Serves 8

WINE RECOMMENDATION: This richly flavored dish matches well with a soft, full-flavored red wine such as Merlot or Pinot Noir.

PER SERVING: 17.7 oz. (497 g.)/ Calories 298/ Total fat 6 g./ Sat. fat 1 g./ Cholesterol 150 mg./ Sodium 410 mg./ Carbohydrate 15 g./ Protein 39 g.

New Year's Eve Seafood Soup
New England
Extra-Lean

Contributed by Tim Delorme, Auburn, Maine.

2   Tbsp. butter
2   Tbsp. flour
4   cups strained lobster stock or fish stock
½   cup lowfat evaporated milk
¼   cup sherry

1   tsp. pepper
1   tsp. thyme
¾   lb. salmon, cut into bite-sized pieces
½   lb. cleaned raw shrimp
2   lbs. mussels, steamed and shucked

Melt butter in medium saucepan. Stir in flour to make a roux. Whisk in lobster stock. Stir occasionally as soup thickens. Add evaporated milk and sherry, pepper and thyme; simmer and stir. Add salmon and cook for five minutes. Add shrimp, cook for an additional five minutes. Add mussels and warm.

Serve with French bread toasted with garlic and Parmesan cheese.

Serves 4-6

WINE RECOMMENDATION: Sherry flavors go well with chilled off-dry white wines such as Riesling or Chenin Blanc.

PER SERVING: 16.5 oz. (463 g.)/ Calories 377/ Total fat 17 g./ Sat. fat 6 g./ Cholesterol 164 mg./ Sodium 750 mg./ Carbohydrate 10 g./ Protein 40 g.

MOLLUSC SOUP
ITALY
Quick-to-Fix ∞ Extra-Lean

IN THE MIDST OF OUR FINAL PREPARATIONS for sending this manuscript to the publisher, a friend from Italy came to visit us here in Maine. Alberto Ferrerri, an Italian military officer assigned to the U.N. Peacekeeping missions around the world, was excited when I told him about our impending mussel cookbook (particularly after sampling Great Eastern's mussels cooked in our favorite sauce of garlic, onions, peppers, olive oil and wine).

Upon returning to Rome he immediately researched a number of his favorite seafood recipes, including several mussel dishes. He translated them all into English, converted the ingredient amounts and suggested appropriate wine pairings. (He recommends Cinque Terres Linguria with this recipe.) After testing several of the mussel dishes we chose three that we found exciting, different and delicious. Enjoy... Salute!
P.S. If you're uncertain about eating octopus, you can substitute squid. (eeeeewwww)

1   lb. littleneck clams, scrubbed and rinsed
1   lb. octopus, chopped in ½-inch slices
¾   lb. red tomatoes
3   cloves minced garlic
2   onions, diced 1½ cup
¼   cup olive oil
1   tsp. black pepper
⅓   cup red wine
2   lbs. mussels
2   Tbsp. parsley

Wash clams and octopus. Dip the whole tomatoes in boiling water for 30 seconds or so, then plunge them into cold water. The skins should peel right off.

In a 6-quart pan over medium heat, sauté the garlic and onion in olive oil until tender. Add tomatoes, octopus, black pepper, and wine. Simmer for 3 minutes.

Add mussels and clams. Simmer for 3 minutes, then stir in parsley. Simmer 3 minutes longer, until shells are all open.

Garnish with lemon wedges if desired. Serve with crusty bread.

Serves 4

WINE RECOMMENDATION: Tomatoes, red wine and black pepper suggest a lusty Cabernet or Merlot that is not too tannic.

PER SERVING: 13.7 oz. (384 g.)/ Calories 350/ Total fat 16 g./ Sat. fat 2 g./ Cholesterol 95 mg./ Sodium 623 mg./ Carbohydrate 15 g./ Protein 31 g.

CHAPTER TEN

∞

ENTRÉES

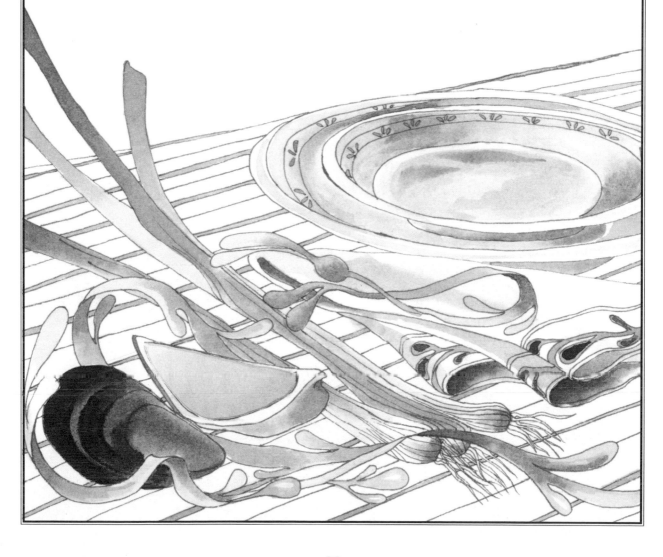

BELGIAN-STYLE MUSSELS
BELGIUM
Low Sodium ⚬ *Quick-to-Fix*

MONTREAL HAS SEVERAL "MOULERIES"— or mussel restaurants patterned after those found in Belgium. One of these is L'Actual, which features seven mussel specials in the shell and six de-shelled mussel dishes, all served with Belgian fries (deep-fried potato wedges).

If you make a trip to Brussels you'll find "Moules et Frits" (Mussels and Fries) on menus all over the city. It is the national dish of Belgium. Mussels cooked with cream and leeks is our interpretation of Belgian-Style Mussels.

1 Tbsp. olive oil	2 Tbsp. white-wine vinegar or tarragon vinegar
1 Tbsp. shallots	½ cup heavy cream
¾ cup leek whites, chopped	dry white wine (optional)
1 cup mushrooms, diced	
2 lbs. mussels	

Heat olive oil in dutch oven or heavy pot and sauté shallots, leeks and mushrooms until limp, but not brown. Add mussels, vinegar and heavy cream. Cover and steam on high about 4 minutes until mussels are opened. Thin sauce with white wine if desired.

Serves 2

WINE RECOMMENDATION: A crisp, clean Chardonnay with a minimum of oak aging would be a nice match.

PER SERVING: 9.3 oz. (262 g.)/ Calories 375/ Total fat 31 g./ Sat. fat. 15 g./ Cholesterol 181 mg./ Sodium 33 mg./ Carbohydrate 14 g./ Protein 14 g.

MUSSELS WITH LINGUINE AND PERFECT SPAGHETTI SAUCE

ITALY

Extra-Lean ∞ *Low-Fat*

Linguine is pasta in long, flat, thin strands.

4 lbs. mussels	2 cups red wine
¼ cup olive oil	1½ Tbsp. oregano
2 onions, thinly sliced	1½ Tbsp. basil
2 cloves garlic, finely minced	⅛ tsp. red pepper
2 lemons, finely sliced	½ tsp. black pepper
2 1 lb. 13 oz. cans Italian tomatoes, mashed	2 tsp. salt
	2 lbs. dried linguine
1 6 oz. can tomato paste	2 Tbsp. olive oil

Steam mussels until shells open then set aside. Sauté onion and garlic in oil in 6-quart kettle. When onion is golden and soft, add lemon slices, tomatoes, tomato paste, wine, oregano, basil, peppers and salt. Cover and simmer over low heat for 25 minutes. Then simmer uncovered until sauce thickens.

Remove top half of shell from cooled mussels, and add meats to sauce. Cover and cook over medium-high heat just long enough to heat mussels.

While mussels are warming, cook linguine according to directions and toss with 2 Tbsp. olive oil to prevent sticking. Cover linguine with mussels and sauce. Serve immediately.

Serves 8-10

WINE RECOMMENDATION: Rich tomato sauces are great with rich, fruity red wines such as California Zinfandel, Australian Shiraz or Italian Chiantis.

PER SERVING: 17.8 oz. (497 g.)/ Calories 281/ Total fat 4 g./ Sat. fat .5 g./ Cholesterol 50 mg./ Sodium 723 mg./ Carbohydrate 43 g./ Protein 12 g.

EASY LINGUINE AND CLAM SAUCE WITH MUSSELS

Quick-to-Fix

2 lbs. mussels

6 Tbsp. butter

4 cloves garlic, chopped

2 8-oz. cans minced or chopped clams

⅓ cup parsley, chopped

1½ Tbsp. cornstarch to thicken

8 oz. fresh linguine

Steam mussels and set aside. After they cool, remove the top shell from half of the batch and just save the meats from the other half. Chop those meats in half.

Melt butter in large fry pan with garlic and sauté for 3 minutes. Add clams (with the clam juice from the can) and parsley. Add chopped mussel meats and stir. If you want thicker sauce, add a little cornstarch mixed with water. Then add the half-shelled mussels to the sauce. Bring to a simmer (avoid overcooking the mussels) and serve over pasta.

Serves 2

WINE RECOMMENDATION: A crisp, clean Sauvignon Blanc is a great choice here.

PER SERVING: 21.5 oz. (603 g.)/ Calories 979/ Total fat 47 g./ Sat. fat 23g./ Cholesterol 473 mg./ Sodium 1084 mg./ Carbohydrate 83 g./ Protein 62 g.

MUSSEL JAMBALAYA

U.S.—CAJUN

Extra-Lean ∞ *Low-Fat*

2	lbs. mussels	2	ribs celery, chopped
1½	cups water	1	cup diced cooked ham, preferably smoked—OR—diced cooked chicken
2	cups chicken broth	2	cups canned Italian plum tomatoes, well drained
2	cups mussel broth	¼	tsp. nutmeg
2	Tbsp. unsalted butter	¼	tsp. ground cloves
2	Tbsp. cooking oil		pepper to taste
1	cup finely chopped onions	¼	tsp. hot sauce
3	cloves garlic, finely chopped	¼	cup freshly chopped parsley
2	cups uncooked long grain rice		
1	green pepper, cored, seeded and chopped		

Steam mussels in 1½ cups water. Cool mussels and shuck, reserving broth. Set meats aside. Mix 2 cups of mussel broth with 2 cups chicken broth and set aside.

In medium stock pot sauté onions and garlic in butter and oil until onion is translucent. Add dry rice, stir carefully, making sure rice kernels are well coated and slightly golden. Add half of the mixed broth, stir and cook over medium heat for about 2 minutes. Add green pepper, celery, ham, tomatoes, spices, and hot sauce. Add remaining 2 cups of mixed broth. Cover and cook over low heat until rice has absorbed the liquid (about 15 minutes). Adjust spices, and add liquid if dish seems dry.

Carefully mix in mussel meats and accumulated juices. Garnish with parsley and serve with warm corn bread.

Serves 4-6

WINE RECOMMENDATION: This rich dish could stand up well to a rich, low-tannin red wine such as Pinot Noir or Italian Chianti.

PER SERVING: 22 oz. (614 g.)/ Calories 617/ Total fat 17 g./ Sat. fat 5 g./ Cholesterol 74 mg./ Sodium 1354 mg./ Carbohydrate 91 g./ Protein 25 g.

PAELLA

SPAIN

THE EXPENSIVE SPICE SAFFRON (from the pistil of a purple-flowered crocus) is said to be the perfect complement to mussels, and is the secret ingredient in paella. It takes 4000 flowers to yield one ounce of spice.

⅓ cup olive oil
1 lb. chicken breasts and small drumsticks
2 cloves garlic, chopped
¾ cup scallions, chopped with green tops
1½ cups tomatoes, chopped
½ cup red bell pepper, cut in strips
2 stalks (½ cup) celery, coarsely chopped
3 cups water
1½ cups long grain rice, uncooked
2 tsp. paprika
1 cube chicken bouillon
1 tsp. turmeric
½ tsp. chili powder
½ tsp. saffron
½ lb. chorizo or hot sausage, sliced or crumbled
1 lb. shrimp, peeled and deveined
2 lbs. mussels
¾ cup canned garbanzo beans, rinsed and drained
1 15-oz. can artichokes, drained and halved
½ cup peas
   salt and pepper to taste

Heat oil in large 6-quart saucepan. Add chicken and cook on all sides until browned (about 15 minutes). Remove and set aside.

Add garlic, scallions, tomatoes, red bell pepper, and celery to pan and sauté until tender, about 5 minutes. Drain excess oil. Add water, rice, paprika, bouillon, turmeric, chili powder, and saffron. Mix well with vegetables.

Add chicken and chorizo, then bring to boil. Reduce heat and simmer covered for 15 minutes. Add shrimp, mussels and garbanzo beans, then simmer 5 more minutes. Finally, add artichokes and peas and simmer a final 5 minutes. Add salt and pepper to taste.

Serve immediately in a "paellero" or shallow-sided casserole dish.

Serves 8-10

WINE RECOMMENDATION: This rich, complex dish would be terrific with a dry, well-chilled California or Spanish sparkling wine.

PER SERVING: 14.5 oz. (405 g.)/ Calories 541/ Total fat 23 g./ Sat. fat 5 g./ Cholesterol 154 mg./ Sodium 748 mg./ Carbohydrate 51 g./ Protein 34 g.

MUSSEL RISOTTO
SPAIN

A risotto is rice cooked in broth with grated cheese and seasonings.

2 lbs. mussels
½ cup white wine
6 Tbsp. butter
1 shallot, finely chopped
1 small onion, finely chopped
3 cloves garlic, crushed
½ tsp. saffron threads dissolved in 2 Tbsp. boiling water

1 cup risotto rice
1 cup mussel broth
1½ cups water
¼ cup Parmesan cheese, grated
    small handful fresh parsley, finely chopped

Steam mussels in ½ cup wine. Allow to cool. Drain broth and reserve. Shuck all but eight of the mussels and put aside.

Melt butter in 6-quart pan. Add the shallot, onion and garlic. Sauté over medium heat until soft. Add saffron and rice to butter mixture and sauté for 2 minutes.

Add 1 cup mussel broth and 1½ cups water. Bring to boil then reduce heat and simmer uncovered for about 20 minutes, stirring occasionally. Rice should absorb most of the broth so it is *al dente* in texture.

Stir in Parmesan cheese and mussel meats. Put risotto into serving dish and garnish with mussels in the shell and parsley.

Serves 4-6

WINE RECOMMENDATION: This rich dish would benefit by the contrast of a crisp, clean white wine such as California Sauvignon Blanc or Italian Orvieto.

PER SERVING: 6.5 oz. (181 g.)/ Calories 434/ Total fat 21 g./ Sat. fat 12 g./ Cholesterol 79 mg./ Sodium 443 mg./ Carbohydrate 43 g./ Protein 14 g.

New England Mussels in a Vermouth/Saffron Sauce

New England

Low Sodium

THIS RECIPE WILL ALWAYS BE SPECIAL to me because my father used to make it for the whole family when we had our relatives over for the traditional Italian Sunday meal. We had a wonderful time enjoying this great dish with our family.

Chef Steve Capodicasa, Fanwood, New Jersey
Note: It is said that mussels and saffron are a "marriage made in heaven."

2 lbs. mussels	1¾ cups sweet Vermouth
1 cup white wine	½ cup heavy cream
1½ cups mussel broth (reserved)	salt
1½ cups water	pepper
8 oz. tomato paste	2 Tbsp. butter
10-12 sprigs thyme (or about 2 Tbsp. fresh thyme)	2 Tbsp. flour
6-8 saffron threads	1⅓ lbs. fresh angel-hair pasta

Steam mussels in wine until opened. Drain 1½ cups broth into 6 quart saucepan. Set mussels aside.

Add water to mussel broth and bring to rolling simmer. Add tomato paste, thyme and ½ of the saffron. Simmer for 10-12 minutes half-covered. Add vermouth and simmer 3-4 minutes longer uncovered. Stir in cream and add remaining saffron threads. Sauce should be light red in color. Add salt and pepper to taste.

Make roux by melting butter and adding flour. Cook on low for 10 minutes, stirring constantly, taking care not to scorch. Whisk roux into sauce until desired thickness is reached. Add mussels and warm through.

Arrange mussels around bowls of pasta and spoon sauce over top.

Serves 4-6

WINE RECOMMENDATIONS: The sweet vermouth flavors match best with an off-dry, slightly sweet wine such as Gewurztraminer or Riesling.

PER SERVING: 19.6 oz. (550 g.)/ Calories 932/ Total fat 23 g./ Sat. fat 12 g./ Cholesterol 255 mg./ Sodium 707 mg./ Carbohydrate 110 g./ Protein 29 g.

CAPE COD TARRAGON FRIED MUSSELS

NEW ENGLAND

THIS RECIPE IS A RESULT of family contributions and a Japanese cookbook. Our son-in-law is a commercial fisherman out of Cape Cod. Once in awhile he'll pick up some local shellfish, or we'll get a basketful while we're out clamming. We found a recipe for fried clams in the Japanese cookbook and used mussels instead. My contribution was the tarragon, a favorite herb with a distinctive flavor that blends well with the mussels.

Zane Rodriguez, Centerville, Massachusetts

2 lbs. mussels
4 egg yolks
¼ tsp. salt
½ tsp. dried tarragon

cornstarch
3 Tbsp. margarine or butter for frying
lemon wedges

Steam and shuck mussels; dry meats on paper towels. Save shells.

Beat egg yolks with salt and tarragon. Dust meats with cornstarch and dip in egg yolk mixture. Fry 1-2 minutes in margarine/butter. Serve in shells with lemon wedges.

Serves 2

WINE RECOMMENDATION: Almost any clean, crisp still or sparkling wine would work here.

PER SERVING: 5.6 oz. (158g.)/ Calories 375/ Total fat 30 g./ Sat. fat. 13 g./ Cholesterol 352 mg./ Sodium 753mg./ Carbohydrate 6 g./ Protein 20 g.

COZZE MONA LISA

ITALY

Extra-Lean

MY DAUGHTER LISA LOVES MUSSELS and could not find a good mussel dish anywhere, so she asked me to create a mussel recipe for her. I put this dish together and she loved it, so I put it on the menu in my ristorante. It became so famous, people come from all over the Philadelphia area to get this dish, which I call "Cozze Mona Lisa."

Gregorio Martine, Bensalem, PA
Note: "Cozze" means "mussels" in Italian.

18 oz. marinara or Perfect Spaghetti Sauce
(p. 85)

8 oz. red chianti wine

3 dashes Tabasco sauce

3 oz. Worcestershire sauce

2 lbs. mussels

Combine all ingredients except mussels in a 4-quart Dutch oven. Cook covered on high until sauce is boiling, then lower heat. Add mussels and simmer 5-6 minutes until mussels open.

Serve immediately over pasta or orzo with Italian garlic bread.

Serves 4

WINE RECOMMENDATION: Chianti of course would be the first choice followed by a California Red Zinfandel.

PER SERVING: 9.5 oz. (255 g.)/ Calories 223/ Total fat 8 g./ Sat. fat 1 g./ Cholesterol 27 mg./ Sodium 1052 mg./ Carbohydrate 18 g./ Protein 10 g.

SALSA-STEAMED MUSSELS
MEXICO
Quick-to-Fix ∞ *Extra-Lean* ∞ *Low-Fat*
Contributed by Gail S. MacDonough, Wayland, Massachusetts

2 lbs. mussels

1 cup white wine

1 10-oz. jar salsa

Pour wine and salsa over mussels and steam in large pot until shells open. Serve as appetizer or with Spanish-style rice as a main course.

Serves 2

WINE RECOMMENDATION: This straightforward dish would go well with a clean, crisp Chardonnay or soft red wine such as Gamay or Pinot Noir. If the salsa used is very hot and spicy, go with a softer white such as Chenin Blanc.

PER SERVING: 13.3 oz. (372 g.)/ Calories 199/ Total fat 2 g./ Sat. fat 0/ Cholesterol 60 mg./ Sodium 1409 mg./ Carbohydrate 9 g./ Protein 15 g.

MUSSELS IN BLUE CHEESE SAUCE
BELGIUM
Quick-to-Fix

M Y HUSBAND returned from a trip to Belgium and raved about a dish of mussels in blue cheese sauce he had eaten in a restaurant there. I figured that since the Belgians are famous for their mussels, it was an idea worth trying. After some experimentation, this recipe was devised.

Elizabeth Masson, Bethesda, Maryland

2 Tbsp. butter
1 carrot, chopped
1 onion, chopped

2 lbs. mussels
1 cup white wine
4 oz. blue cheese, crumbled

Sauté carrot and onion in butter in saucepan. Add mussels and wine and cook on medium heat until mussels open, shaking pan occasionally. Remove mussels to serving dish.

Add blue cheese to cooking broth. Stir over medium heat until cheese melts. Pour sauce over mussels and serve.

Serves 2

WINE RECOMMENDATION: A rich barrel-fermented and aged Chardonnay would be great with a creamy blue cheese.

PER SERVING: 13 oz. (364 g.)/ Calories 508/ Total fat 30 g./ Sat. fat 18 g./ Cholesterol 130 mg./ Sodium 1212 mg./ Carbohydrate 13 g./ Protein 28 g.

SEAFOOD FRA DIAVOLO

ITALY

Extra-Lean ∞ *Low-Fat*

I SPENT MANY SUMMERS at Montauk, New York. This is a takeoff of my favorite dish served there at the Surfside Restaurant.

Sandra J. Leonard, Fairborn, Ohio

2	Tbsp. olive oil
2	garlic cloves, minced fine
1	onion, minced medium fine
4	cups crushed canned tomatoes
2	Tbsp. freshly chopped parsley
½	tsp. oregano leaves, crushed

1	tsp. basil, dried
¼	tsp. hot red pepper flakes, crushed
	salt and pepper to taste
2	lbs. mussels
1	lb. shrimp, peeled and deveined
2	lbs. fresh linguine pasta

Sauté garlic and onion in olive oil 2-3 minutes. Add crushed tomatoes, parsley, oregano, basil and hot pepper flakes. Stir well. Simmer for one hour covered. Add salt and pepper to taste. Add mussels and cover. When mussels start to open, add shrimp and continue to cook 5 minutes.

Serve over hot linguine.

Serves 6

WINE RECOMMENDATION: Rich tomato sauces are great with low-tannin reds such as Italian Chianti or California Pinot Noirs.

PER SERVING: 15.3 oz (429 g.)/ Calories 655/ Total fat 13 g./ Sat. fat 3 g./ Cholesterol 307 mg./ Sodium 864 mg./ Carbohydrate 97 g./ Protein 38 g.

MUSSELS WITH SHIITAKE MUSHROOMS
REGIONAL U.S.
Low Sodium

WE FIRST FELL IN LOVE with mussels at a restaurant serving a dish similar to this one. At the end of the meal we complimented our server on how great the mussels tasted, this being our first time trying them. She told us that most people who order this dish leave the mussels on the side of the plate, having never even tasted them!

Glen & Christine Groves, Ocala, Florida

1 lb. fresh fettucine noodles
2 lbs. mussels
1 8-oz. bottle clam juice
1 Tbsp. white wine
1 Tbsp. fresh lemon juice
1 Tbsp. cornstarch

1 cup cream or half-and-half
2 Tbsp. butter or olive oil
3 oz. fresh shiitake mushrooms
1 small onion
6 cloves crushed garlic
2 Tbsp. minced parsley

Serves 4-6

Freezes very well.

Cook noodles per package directions.

Steam mussels with clam juice, wine and lemon juice until they pop open. Take mussels out of shells and put in a covered bowl.

Pour liquid into smaller pan, straining out sediment. Cook liquid until reduced by half. In separate bowl, stir cornstarch into cream and add to the liquid in the pot. Cook until thickened.

Slice mushrooms and onion into quarter-inch strips. Sauté mushrooms, onion and garlic a few minutes in the butter/olive oil and add to cream sauce. Add mussel meats and parsley. Heat to bubbling. Serve over cooked fettucine.

WINE RECOMMENDATION: The earthy flavor of shiitakes along with the rich cream sauce really demand a rich, barrel-aged Chardonnay.

PER SERVING: 12.4 oz. (346 g.)/ Calories 693/ Total fat 35 g./ Sat. fat 16 g./ Cholesterol 225 mg./ Sodium 338 mg./ Carbohydrate 73 g./ Protein 23 g.

MUSSEL MOUSSAKA
GREECE

2 lbs. mussels
¼ cup white wine
2 large eggplants, sliced
1 large onion, chopped
¼ cup olive oil
2 cups tomato sauce
½ tsp. garlic powder
  salt and pepper to taste

SAUCE

6 Tbsp. butter
1 cup milk or light cream
3 eggs, beaten
¼ cup flour

Steam mussels in white wine. Allow to cool. Drain. Shuck the mussels and put meats aside. Save a few shells for side plate garnish if desired.

Lightly salt eggplant slices, and place on absorbent paper for ten minutes, then press between paper towels to remove excess liquids.

Sauté eggplant slices and onion in the oil until lightly browned. Remove eggplant to brown paper to drain. Drain onions in sieve.

Combine in 4-quart baking dish the eggplant, onion, mussels, tomato sauce, garlic powder, salt and pepper. Stir to blend evenly. Set dish aside.

To make sauce, melt butter over low heat. Add flour. Remove from heat. Add beaten eggs and milk or cream. Pour egg mixture over eggplant and bake at 350 degrees for 30 minutes.

Serves 4

WINE RECOMMENDATION: This rich dish has lots of flavors which suggest a contrast of a crisp, clean white wine such as a California Sauvignon Blanc, Italian Orvieto or any other simple, fresh wine.

PER SERVING: 25 oz. (699 g.)/ Calories 655/ Total fat 42 g./ Sat. fat 16 g./ Cholesterol 402 mg./ Sodium 1013 mg./ Carbohydrate 44 g./ Protein 26 g.

MAINE STOVETOP LOBSTER BAKE
NEW ENGLAND
Low Sodium

AT THE 1994 INTERNATIONAL BOSTON SEAFOOD SHOW, our booth was positioned next to that of the Maine Lobster Promotional Council. Since Maine lobster has a terrific reputation, and since more and more lobster/clambakes are using mussels instead of clams, we decided to develop a stovetop lobster bake with mussels. This recipe works well with slices of kielbasa sausage added.

You can use a very large lobster pot or dutch oven, as well as a roasting pan. Be sure the pan doesn't have a scooped bottom that won't allow it to make contact with the burners or grill.

8   small boiling onions
12 small red potatoes
4   ears sweet corn
5   lbs. rockweed (seaweed). If unavailable, add 2 Tbsp. salt to water and a rack to lift lobster off the bottom of the pan so it doesn't scorch

4   1¼-lb. Maine lobsters
4   lbs. mussels
2   cups water
1½ sticks butter, melted
2   lemons, cut into wedges

Parboil onions and potatoes. Partially shuck corn, leaving innermost husks. In a large (12" x 16") roasting pan, place a one-inch layer of seaweed. Put lobsters on top of seaweed and arrange corn and onions between lobsters and the sides of the pan. Place more seaweed over lobster and gently add mussels and potatoes, being careful to keep the top of the Bake level. Cover with remaining seaweed and add the water to the pan.

Cover tightly with lid or foil and place on stove or a preheated grill to cook. (If using a grill make sure coals are very hot.) Start timing when you first see steam. Cook covered for 15 minutes.

Serve with melted butter and lemon wedges on the side.

Serves 4

WINE RECOMMENDATION: Lobster has a buttery, sweet flavor that goes wonderfully with a rich Chardonnay from California, France or even Chile.

PER SERVING: 33 oz. (921 g.)/ Calories 886/ Total fat 41 g./ Sat. fat 22 g./ Cholesterol 292 mg./ Sodium 666 mg./ Carbohydrate 86 g./ Protein 52 g.

LATITUDES MUSSELS MADEIRA

NEW ENGLAND

Low Sodium

Contributed by Tom Snowe, Latitudes Restaurant, Auburn, Maine

2 lbs. mussels
¼ cup white wine
4 Tbsp. butter
½ cup onions
1 cup mushrooms

½ cup Madeira wine
1 Tbsp. maple syrup
1 cup light cream
4 servings wild rice, cooked

Steam mussels in white wine and shuck when cool. Save a few shells for garnish.

Sauté onions and mushrooms in butter until tender. Add Madeira and simmer 3 minutes to reduce it. Add maple syrup and blend. Add cream and simmer until it thickens. Serve over wild rice.

Serves 4

WINE RECOMMENDATION: The sweetness from the Madeira and maple syrup would connect nicely with an off-dry, slightly sweet Riesling, Chenin Blanc or even an "extra dry" or "demi-see" sparkling wine or champagne.

PER SERVING: 9.5 oz. (268 g.)/ Calories 376/ Total fat 21 g./ Sat. fat 12 g./ Cholesterol 93 mg./ Sodium 223 mg./ Carbohydrate 27 g./ Protein 12 g.

STIR-FRY MUSSELS

THAILAND

AFTER SPENDING SEVERAL WEEKS IN THAILAND in 1990, I became quite fond of the food and the wonderful herbs and spices that gave it a sweet, sour, citrus, clean flavor. And it was low fat. Returning as chef of the Belmont, I wanted to combine these flavors with local seafood.

Jerry Clare, chef, The Belmont Inn and Restaurant, Camden, ME

3 Tbsp. oil
4 Tbsp. fermented black beans
2 Tbsp. Thai chili paste
4 Tbsp. hoisin sauce
2 Tbsp. fresh ginger, minced
2 Tbsp. lemon grass, minced
1 Tbsp. sugar

2 lbs. mussels
1 Tbsp. Thai fish sauce
   juice of 1 lime
2 Tbsp. red bell pepper, minced, for garnish
1 cup scallions, cut on slant
2 Tbsp. fresh cilantro, chopped

In a large sauté pan heat the oil over high heat. Add the black beans, chili paste, hoisin sauce, ginger, lemon grass, and sugar. Cook one minute, stirring to blend all ingredients. Add mussels all at once, shaking the pan to coat them. Add the fish sauce and lime juice into the pan. Cover and cook for five minutes until the shells have opened. Pour onto a large platter and garnish with red pepper, scallions, and cilantro.

Serves 6

WINE RECOMMENDATION: Spicy, Thai-style dishes are wonderful with a good off-dry Gewurztraminer, or for contrast a crisp, sparkling wine.

PER SERVING: 3.2 oz. (89 g.) Calories 144/Total fat 7 g./ Sat. fat 1 g./ Cholesterol 19 mg./ Sodium 371 mg./ Carbohydrate 14 g./ Protein 8 g.

LEBANON'S BOWL OF RICE

Extra-Lean ∞ *Low-Fat*

Contributed by Alberto Ferrerri, Rome, Italy

1 lb. littleneck clams, scrubbed and rinsed	¼ cup brandy
2 lbs. mussels	reserved mussel broth
1¼ cups long-grain rice	1 tsp. black pepper
2 Tbsp. olive oil	1 Tbsp. minced fresh basil
2 cloves garlic	¾ cup chopped onion
⅔ lb. medium shrimp, peeled and deveined.	dash Worcestershire sauce (optional)
⅔ lb. Maine (small) shrimp, peeled	lemon wedges for garnish
juice of one lemon	

Steam clams for 2 minutes, then add mussels and continue to steam for 4 more minutes until the shells open. Drain and reserve broth. Shuck clams and mussels, saving a few shells for garnish.

Cook rice until done; put aside and keep warm.

In 6-quart saucepan, sauté the garlic in olive oil until golden, then add medium shrimp and cook over medium heat for one minute, then add the small shrimp and sauté one more minute. Squeeze lemon over the shrimp and add the brandy, sautéing another minute longer.

Add mussel and clam meats, ½ cup of the reserved broth, and black pepper. Simmer 2 minutes. Add basil and onion. Simmer 1 minute longer, then add rice. Mix thoroughly. Transfer to serving dish and sprinkle with Worcestershire sauce. Garnish with shells and lemon wedges if desired.

Serves 2-4

WINE RECOMMENDATION: This straightforward dish really brings the flavor of the mussels to the fore. Try a crisp, clean Sauvignon Blanc. (Alberto Ferrerri recommends Pinot Bianco.)

PER SERVING: 11.6 oz. (326 g.)/ Calories 507/ Total fat 9 g./ Sat. fat 1 g./ Cholesterol 252 mg./ Sodium 732 mg./ Carbohydrate 53 g./ Protein 42 g.

Mussel Putanesca Pizza Sauce

Italy

Extra-Lean

VARIATION: Doctor up a frozen pizza by adding mussel meats and black olives instead of adding pepperoni or sausage, and you'll have a more heart-healthy pizza. You can use prepared pizza dough, or you can make ours.

PIZZA DOUGH (FOR 2 PIZZA PANS OR COOKIE SHEETS):

- 1 cup warm water (110-115 degrees)
- 1 pk. active dry yeast
- 2½–3 cups unbleached flour
- 2 Tbsp. olive oil
- ½ tsp. salt

SAUCE:

- 2 lbs. mussels
- ¼ cup white wine
- ¾ cup finely chopped onion
- 2 cloves minced garlic
- 2 Tbsp. olive oil

- 1 28-oz. can tomatoes, coarsely chopped, with liquid
- 1 tsp. dried oregano
- 1 tsp. dried basil
- 1 bay leaf
  black pepper, to taste
- 1 tsp. red pepper flakes
- ½ cup mussel broth
- ½ cup red wine
- 1 2 oz. can anchovies, drained, finely chopped
- 2 Tbsp. capers
- 18 pitted black olives, sliced or crushed
- ½ cup fresh Parmesan cheese, shredded

TO MAKE DOUGH: combine water and yeast in a large mixing bowl, stirring well. Allow to set for 2 minutes. Add half the flour, the olive oil, and the salt to the yeast mixture. Combine well. Gradually add the remaining flour until dough becomes sticky, but not so sticky that it won't pull away from the bowl easily.

Turn dough out onto a floured board and knead, slowly dusting with flour to make dough workable and not sticky.

Coat a separate bowl with olive oil and add dough to bowl, turning so as to lightly coat dough surface. Set bowl and dough in warm area, cover with a damp towel, and allow to rise until doubled (about 1½ to 2 hours).

Remove dough from bowl and punch down. Grease the pizza pans well with olive oil. Divide dough in half and roll out until slightly larger than the pans. Allow to rest a minute, then place in the pans. Top and bake according to recipe instructions.

FOR SAUCE: Steam mussels in white wine. Cool, drain and reserve broth. Shuck mussels and reserve meats, saving a few shells for garnish if desired.

Using a 3-quart saucepan over medium heat,

sauté the garlic and onion in the olive oil until tender. Add tomatoes and their liquid, oregano, basil, bay leaf, and peppers. Simmer for 3 minutes, stirring to prevent sticking.

Add reserved mussel broth, red wine, anchovies, capers and black olives. Simmer uncovered for 30 minutes. When sauce has simmered to desired consistency, top your favorite pizza dough with half the sauce and bake in a 425-degree oven for 8 minutes. Remove pizza and top with rest of sauce, then add mussel meats and sprinkle with Parmesan. Return to oven and bake 8 more minutes.

Makes 2 pizzas

WINE RECOMMENDATION: Tomatoes, olives and herbs along with the zing of hot chiles would go well with a spicy Zinfandel or young fresh Cabernet.

PER SERVING: 6.1 oz. (171 g.)/ Calories 241/ Total fat 8 g./ Sat. fat 2 g./ Cholesterol 17 mg./ Sodium 645 mg./ Carbohydrate 30 g./ Protein 10 g.

DELICIOUS DESPERATION
Quick-to-Fix ∞ Extra-Lean

THIS IS SUCH A FAST RECIPE TO PREPARE. Mussels take five minutes, as does the fresh pasta and the sauce, so it is perfect for the person who wants a quick meal. Thus the name "Delicious Desperation."

2 lbs. mussels
14 oz. fresh pasta, spaghetti or linguine

14 oz. prepared spaghetti sauce

Steam mussels until opened.

Boil pasta according to package directions. (Fresh pasta takes about half the cooking time as dried pasta.) Add the cooked mussels in the shell to a simmering spaghetti sauce and just cook until mussels are heated through, about a minute.

Serve over pasta.

Serves 2

WINE RECOMMENDATION: If you're using a rich tomato-based sauce with lots of spices and herbs, by all means try a robust California Zinfandel with this dish.

PER SERVING: 17.7 oz. (496 g.)/ Calories 876/ Total fat 19 g./ Sat. fat 2 g./ Cholesterol 277 mg./ Sodium 2030 mg./ Carbohydrate 138 g./ Protein 41 g.

CHAPTER ELEVEN

SALADS AND BRUNCH

SUMMER DREAM SEA SALAD
REGIONAL U.S.

Note: the little squid tentacles look kind of cute in this colorful dish
Richard Wood and Cathy Silvey, Mercer Island, Washington

2   lbs. mussels
½   cup white wine
⅔   lb. fresh whole squid (10-12 squid)
⅓   cup olive oil
    juice of 2 lemons
2   Tbsp. fresh chopped mint leaves
2   cloves garlic, mashed
½   tsp. black pepper
1   tsp. fresh thyme, chopped fine
⅔   lb. medium shrimp, shelled, deveined,
    cooked and chilled

VEGETABLES:
2   carrots, shredded
1   green pepper, julienned
½   red pepper, julienned
½   yellow pepper, julienned
½   red onion, sliced
½   lb. water chestnuts, sliced
½   cup fresh chopped parsley
½   cup black olives, sliced

Steam mussels in ½ cup wine. Cool and shuck half of mussels. Put unshucked mussels in refrigerator, to add later.

Clean squid—separate bodies from heads. Remove innards and cuttle bone from bodies; cut tentacles from heads just above the eyes. Remove beaks. Slice bodies into rings; chop up tentacles. (EEEEE-WWW! Buy them already cut up if you can! It's called calamari.) Poach gently in water 3 minutes until squid turns white. Remove and add to shelled mussels.

Add olive oil, lemon juice and mint to shucked mussels and squid. Blend well and let marinate for 2 hours or overnight.

Remove squid and mussels from marinade.

Combine garlic, black pepper, and fresh thyme and add to marinade.

In large bowl, combine shrimp and marinated squid and mussels, vegetables, dressing and olives. Toss. Add reserved mussels in shells.

Serves 6 to 8

WINE RECOMMENDATION: Lemony herbal flavors here are a natural with Sauvignon Blanc.

PER SERVING: 11.4 oz. (318 g.)/ Calories 352/ Total fat 17 g./ Sat. fat. 2 g./ Cholesterol 198 mg./ Sodium 510 mg./ Carbohydrate 27 g./ Protein 25 g.

Mediterranean Mussel and Pasta Salad
Italy

DRESSING:

- ⅓ cup olive oil
- 2 Tbsp. lemon juice
- ½ tsp. garlic powder
- 1½ tsp. dried basil
- 1½ tsp. fresh parsley
- salt and pepper to taste

Combine all dressing ingredients and set aside.

Steam mussels in white wine until opened. Cool, drain, and shuck mussels. Set meats aside; save a few shells for garnish if desired.

Cook pasta. Drain and cool.

Combine vegetables, pasta, mussel meats, and dressing in large bowl. Toss and serve.

- 2 lbs. mussels
- ¼ cup white wine
- 1 cup multi-colored rotini, uncooked
- 1 large red bell pepper, ¼-inch dice
- 1 medium onion, ¼-inch dice
- ¾ cup frozen peas
- ¼ cup black olives, sliced

Serves 4-6

WINE RECOMMENDATION: A fresh, "grassy-style" Sauvignon Blanc is a great choice with this dish.

PER SERVING: 8 oz. (222 g.)/ Calories 439/ Total fat 23 g./ Sat. fat 3 g./ Cholesterol 28 mg./ Sodium 561 mg./ Carbohydrate 48 g./ Protein 17 g.

YUCATAN MUSSEL SALAD

MEXICO

Low Sodium ∞ *Quick-to-Fix* ∞ *Extra-Lean*

Courtesy Chef Kerry Altiero, Cafe Miranda, Rockland, Maine

2 lbs. mussels, steamed and shucked	⅓ cup diced red onion
½ cup diced sweet red pepper	¼ cup chopped cilantro
⅓ cup diced green pepper	¾ cup olive oil
1 minced jalapeño pepper	¼ cup lime juice
⅓ cup chopped celery	salt and pepper to taste

Thoroughly mix meats with rest of ingredients and let marinate overnight. Makes 2 lbs. salad.

Serves 4

WINE RECOMMENDATION: The tart, spicy-hot flavors of this dish suggest an off-dry, fruity California Riesling, Gewurztraminer, or even a blush wine like White Zinfandel.

PER SERVING: 5 oz. (143 g.)/ Calories 116/ Total fat 6 g./ Sat. fat 1 g./ Cholesterol 57 mg./ Sodium 22 mg./ Carbohydrate 9 g./ Protein 7 g.

Easy Mussel Salad in Avocado
Regional U.S.
Quick-to-Fix
Contributed by Terence Callery, National Sales Rep, Great Eastern

2 lbs. mussels, cooked and shucked
½ cup diced red pepper
½ cup sliced celery

4 Tbsp. chopped fresh parsley
½ cup creamy Italian salad dressing
3 avocados, cut in half with pit removed

Mix and let marinate overnight. Serve inside a scooped-out avocado.

Serves 6

Wine Recommendation: Almost any crisp, clean, non-oaked white wine would be delicious with this dish.

Per Serving: 8.6 oz. (242 g.)/ Calories 350/ Total fat 24 g./ Sat. fat 4 g./ Cholesterol 19 mg./ Sodium 462 mg./ Carbohydrate 29 g./ Protein 10 g.

Cold English Mussel Salad
England
Low Sodium ∞ Quick-to-Fix

2 lbs. mussels, cooked and shucked
Juice of ½ lemon
⅓ cup mayonnaise
⅓ cup sour cream
3 Tbsp. fresh chopped dill

4 Tbsp. fresh chopped parsley
4 Tbsp. fresh chopped scallions
3 red or green bell peppers cut in half lengthwise, with core and seeds removed

Mix all but peppers and let marinate overnight. Serve inside a half of a red or green pepper.

Serves 6

Wine Recommendation: Herbal flavors are a natural with a good Fumé/Sauvignon Blanc.

Per Serving: 5.7 oz. (159 g.)/ Calories 179/ Total fat 15 g./ Sat. fat 4 g./ Cholesterol 29 mg./ Sodium 169 mg./ Carbohydrate 9 g./ Protein 6 g.

MEL'S MUSSEL FRITTATA

REGIONAL U.S.

Low Sodium

Contributed by Mel Pell, New York, NY

Great Eastern's corporate chef in 1980s

A FRITTATA IS A BAKED OMELETTE that is prepared "unfolded" and finished under a broiler or in a very hot oven.

2	lbs. mussels
¼	cup white wine
1	Tbsp. olive oil
½	broccoli flowerettes, trimmed small
½	medium sweet red pepper, sliced thinly

½	cup scallions, chopped
4	servings (1 lb.) cooked angel-hair pasta
8	eggs, lightly beaten
2	Tbsp. Parmesan cheese, grated

Steam mussels in wine. Allow to cool. Drain. Shuck mussels and set aside. Save a few shells for plate garnish if desired.

In non-stick skillet, saute broccoli, red pepper and scallions in olive oil until cooked al dente (crunchy). Add mussel meats and angel hair pasta. Toss together. Add eggs and cheese, then cook until set. Finish under broiler for 1½ to 2 minutes until lightly browned on top.

Garnish with shells if desired.

Serves 4 as brunch entrée or 8 as an appetizer.

WINE RECOMMENDATION: The richness of eggs and cheese suggests a chilled, dry sparkling wine to add contrast.

PER SERVING: 12.8 oz. (358 g.)/ Calories 829/ Total fat 31 g./ Sat. fat 9 g./ Cholesterol 1007 mg./ Sodium 542 mg./ Carbohydrate 85 g./ Protein 52 g.

MUSSEL QUICHE
FRANCE

THIS RECIPE WAS CREATED at a small, not very well known Mexican/eclectic restaurant in Auburn, Maine. During the final months before this restaurant disappeared from the city, the slightly eccentric owner and his assistant started creating many dishes utilizing mussels because they were so versatile.

One afternoon while they were playing around with mussels, a bowl of steamed mussel meats tipped into the frying batter. After picking the mussels out and putting them in a bowl, the owner noticed the egg pooled up around the meats and got the idea to include them in a quiche. Well, after slight modification to a favorite quiche recipe which the restaurant was noted for, the resulting recipe was a delicious hit.

Tom Snowe, chef, Latitudes Restaurant, Auburn, Maine

2 lbs. mussels	5 eggs
¼ cup white wine	1¼ cups light cream
1 Tbsp. olive oil	1¼ cups whole milk
1 med. onion, thinly sliced	¼ tsp. salt
pastry shell for 10" springform pan	½ tsp. black pepper
1 lb. bacon, cooked until crisp	½ tsp. seasoning salt
1 cup Monterey Jack cheese, shredded	½ tsp. nutmeg

Steam mussels in white wine. Cool, drain and shuck. Save a few shells for garnish if desired.

Sauté onions in olive oil until transparent. Line springform pan (or deep pie pan) with pastry, pressing firmly into seams of pan. Crumble bacon into small pieces and sprinkle evenly over pastry. Sprinkle cheese over the bacon, and layer mussel meats over cheese. Top with sautéed onions.

Preheat oven to 425 degrees. In separate bowl, beat eggs. Add remaining ingredients and mix well. Pour egg mixture over onions, mussels, cheese and bacon. Bake for 15 minutes at 425 degrees, then reduce heat to 375 and bake 40 minutes more. Top

should feel slightly firm when done.

Garnish with a little grated nutmeg and the mussel shells.

Serves 6 to 8

WINE RECOMMENDATION: This rich dish would go well with a crisp Chardonnay that hasn't spent too much time in oak.

PER SERVING: 10.3 oz. (288 g.)/ Calories 765/ Total fat 57 g./ Sat. fat 21 g./ Cholesterol 471 mg./ Sodium 1195 mg./ Carbohydrate 28 g./ Protein 32 g.

CURRIED MUSSELS ON ENGLISH MUFFINS
REGIONAL U.S
Quick-to-Fix

Courtesy Joe Mortensen, Ocean Pride Seafood Company, Salt Lake City, Utah

2   lbs. mussels
⅓   cup white wine
2   Tbsp. butter
1   medium onion, chopped
1   stalk celery, chopped
1   tsp. curry powder

¼   tsp. fresh thyme, finely chopped
⅓   cup mussel broth (reserved)
⅓   cup sour cream
      salt and pepper to taste
4   English muffins, toasted

Steam mussels in ¼ cup of the wine. Cool and shuck, reserving broth—about ⅓ cup. Save a few shells for garnish if desired.

Melt butter in sauce pan. Add onion, celery, and curry powder. Sauté 3 minutes, then add remaining ¼ cup wine and thyme. Add broth and reduce 5 minutes on high. Stir in sour cream, mussel meats, salt and pepper.

Serve over toasted English muffin halves. Garnish with shells and sprig of thyme if desired.

Serves 4

WINE RECOMMENDATION: Curries are great with off-dry, fruity Gewurztraminers and sparkling wines from California and Italy.

PER SERVING: 7.1 oz. (199 g.)/ Calories 329/ Total fat 12 g./ Sat. fat 6 g./ Cholesterol 52 mg./ Sodium 636 mg./ Carbohydrate 36 g./ Protein 13 g.

MUSSEL CRÊPES
FRANCE

CRÊPES ARE EASY TO MAKE, but tedious, as they are thin and must be cooked one at a time. As a shortcut, you can buy them frozen, but the effort to make them from scratch is well worth it.

Contributed by Alberto Ferrerri, Rome, Italy

CRÊPES:
- ¾ cup flour
- 2 Tbsp. sugar
- 1 tsp. salt
- ¾ cup whipping cream
- 3 eggs

FILLING:
- 2 lbs. mussels
- 1¼ cups white wine
- 4 Tbsp. butter
- 1 Tbsp. flour
- 1 med. onion, thinly sliced
- 2 Tbsp. parsley, chopped
- salt and pepper to taste
- 1 cup shredded provolone cheese (optional)

For crêpes, combine ingredients and beat until batter is smooth. Butter a well-warmed 6-8" sauté pan. Add 2 Tbsp. batter, immediately swirling pan to spread batter evenly over bottom. Lightly brown each side then stack on plate and keep warm. Allow 30 to 45 minutes to make 16 crêpes.

For filling, steam mussels in ¼ cup wine. Cool, drain, and shuck, setting the meats aside. Save a few shells for garnish if desired.

Create a roux for thickening by melting 1 Tbsp. of the butter in small saucepan, then stirring in 1 Tbsp. flour. Cook over low heat 2 minutes, stirring constantly. Set aside.

In sauce pan, sauté onion in 2 Tbsp. butter until golden. Add remaining cup of wine and allow to simmer about a minute. Thicken by stirring in roux a little at a time while simmering until creamy thickness is reached. Reduce heat. Add mussel meats, parsley, and remaining butter. Stir to blend.

Put 2 tablespoons of stuffing into each crêpe and roll up. Serve warm. Top with shredded provolone cheese, if desired. Broil lightly to melt.

Makes 12 - 16 crêpes

WINE RECOMMENDATION: This rich dish would go well with a contrasting white wine that was very crisp, clean and refreshing, such as Sauvignon Blanc or Chardonnay.

PER SERVING: 2.6 oz. (72 g.)/ Calories 143/ Total fat 9 g./ Sat. fat 5 g./ Cholesterol 107 mg./ Sodium 227 mg./ Carbohydrate 8 g./ Protein 5 g.

Cindy McIntyre

Cindy McIntyre came to Maine in 1993, after living for 17 years in Tacoma, Washington. She produced her first book in 1987, *Seattle, Tacoma and the Puget Sound Region* (Sammamish Press, Issaquah, WA) and did photography for the large-format coffee table book *Tacoma* a year later. She lives with her son Ryan in the fishing village of Port Clyde.

Terence Callery

Terence Callery has worked for Great Eastern Mussel Farms for eight years as national sales representative. He and his wife Bonnie have a home in Rockland, Maine where they do a lot of gourmet cooking. He holds a Bachelor's Degree in Philosophy from Yale University, and was involved in fundraising and public relations before moving to his wife's home state.

John Ash

Wine expert John Ash is one of California's most influential chefs, named as one of *Food and Wine Magazine's* "hot new chefs of 1985." Condé Nast's *Traveler* called his restaurant, John Ash & Co. "one of the 50 U.S. restaurants worth the journey in 1991," and the *Wine Spectator* described him as "king of the culinary mountain in Sonoma County." To help Fetzer Vineyards launch its food and wine educational programs, Ash became Culinary Director of the Valley Oaks Food & Wine Center in 1990. His steadfast support of local organic farmers has stimulated the growth of many cottage industries that supply restaurants, specialty food shops and markets.

He is the author of *American Game Cooking,* and is now at work on his second book, *From the Garden to the Table: John Ash's Wine Country Cuisine.*

Jerri Finch

Belfast, Maine artist Jerri Finch specializes in quilts and large-scale painted fabric landscapes. Her work has been featured in many publications and exhibitions, and mussels frequently show up in her works.

Patricia Hart

Dietician Patricia Hart has 20 years' combined experience in food preparation, nutrition, food chemistry, sanitation and medicine. A passionate and enthusiastic teacher, she is a part-time instructor at San Francisco State University and gives lectures to professional organizations on nutrition topics. She has won the American Culinary Federation bronze medal for hot food competition, and was awarded Outstanding Student in Wines at the Culinary Institute of America.

INDEX

∞